First Time Voter

Navigating Your Way Through U.S. Elections

Wendi Martin

© **Copyright 2024 - All rights reserved.**

The content contained within this book may not be reproduced, duplicated or transmitted without direct written permission from the author or the publisher.

Under no circumstances will any blame or legal responsibility be held against the publisher, or author, for any damages, reparation, or monetary loss due to the information contained within this book, either directly or indirectly.

Legal Notice:

This book is copyright protected. It is only for personal use. You cannot amend, distribute, sell, use, quote or paraphrase any part, or the content within this book, without the consent of the author or publisher.

Disclaimer Notice:

Please note the information contained within this document is for educational and entertainment purposes only. All effort has been executed to present accurate, up to date, reliable, complete information. No warranties of any kind are declared or implied. Readers acknowledge that the author is not engaged in the rendering of legal, financial, medical or professional advice. The content within this book has been derived from various sources. Please consult a licensed professional before attempting any techniques outlined in this book.

By reading this document, the reader agrees that under no circumstances is the author responsible for any losses, direct or indirect, that are incurred as a result of the use of the information contained within this document, including, but not limited to, errors, omissions, or inaccuracies.

Table of Contents

INTRODUCTION 1

CHAPTER 1: UNDERSTANDING POLITICAL IDEOLOGIES 7

LIBERALISM VS. CONSERVATISM 7
    Liberalism 8
    Conservatism 8
    Real-World Examples 9
    Mutual Criticism 10
    Origins and Landmarks 11
PROGRESSIVISM AND SOCIAL CHANGE 12
    Revolution 13
    Progressivism 14
    Revolutionary and Progressive Movements in History 14
    Arguments in Favor and Against 15
    Examples 16
THE RISE OF POPULISM 18
    Different Approaches of Populism 19
    The Core Characteristics of Populism 20
    The Evolution of American Populism 21
FEMINISM AND GENDER POLITICS 22
    The Evolution of Feminist Movements 22
    Patriarchy 23
    From Suffragettes to Contemporary Advocacy 24
    Gender Gap 25
    Gender Policies 26
    Driving Change: Feminist Strategies in Contemporary Politics 26
    Conservative Critiques of Feminism 27

CHAPTER 2: UNRAVELING THE POLITICAL PARTIES SYSTEM 31

UNDERSTANDING POLITICAL PARTIES 31
    Political Parties vs. Social Organizations 31
    The Crucial Role of Political Parties in Modern Democracies 33
    Understanding Political Party Systems 36
THE ROLE OF THIRD-PARTY CANDIDATES 39
    Third-Party Importance 40
    Third-Party Rise and System Disruption 41
    Historical Examples of Third-Party Emergence 41

    Representative Third Parties in Modern Political Systems 42
  POLITICAL PARTY IDEOLOGIES 43
    Right-Wing Parties 43
    Left-Wing Parties 43
    Center Parties 44
    Anarchist Parties 44
    Democrats and Republicans 44
    Examples 45
    Analyzing Parties in the United States 45

CHAPTER 3: NAVIGATING THE ELECTORAL PROCESS 47

  THE ELECTIONS 47
    Eligibility for U.S. Elections 49
    Constitutional Balance: Republic and Democracy in the United States 50
    The Three Powers: Structure of the United States Republican System 53
  THE ELECTORAL COLLEGE DEBATE 54
    Structure and Function 55
    Winner-Takes-All System 56
  THE PRIMARIES AND CAUCUSES UNVEILED 58
    Caucuses 59
  BALLOT MEASURES AND REFERENDUMS 60
    Initiatives 60
    Referendums 60
    Recalls 60
    Real-Life Examples 61
  POLITICAL POLLING 62
  THE FUTURE OF ELECTION TECHNOLOGY 63
    Comparison of Electronic and Traditional Voting 63
    Advantages and Disadvantages 63
    Risk of Fraud and Historical Examples 64
    Costs and Logistics 64

CHAPTER 4: DOWN-BALLOT VOTING 67

  THE DIVERSITY OF DOWN-BALLOT RACES 68
    Local Races 68
    State Races 68
    Judicial Races 68
  FACTORS SHAPING VOTER CHOICES 69
  THE IMPACT OF DOWN-BALLOT VOTING ON DEMOCRACY 70
  EMPOWERING VOTERS IN DOWN-BALLOT RACES 71
  CASE STUDIES AND SUCCESS STORIES 72

CHAPTER 5: THE EVOLUTION OF POLITICAL CAMPAIGNS 75

POLITICAL MILESTONES THROUGHOUT AMERICAN HISTORY 75
THE EVOLUTION OF AMERICAN POLITICAL PARTIES 78
- The Dual Nature of American Politics 78
- The Dynamics of Alternating Power 78
- Timeline of Political Party Evolution in the United States 79
- Presidents of the United States: Terms, Parties, and Congressional Landscape 81
- America's Dual-Party Landscape: Origins and Implication 86
- Third Parties in the United States: A History of Struggle and Influence 86

POLITICAL PARTY PLATFORMS 88
- Exploring America's Political Spectrum 88
- Timeline of U.S. Political Party Platform Evolution 89

CAMPAIGN FINANCE 92
- The Cost of Electoral Campaigns 92
- Who Regulates the Financing of U.S. Elections? 93
- American Election Financing Process 93
- Sources of Funding for US Elections 94
- Limits on Financial Contributions Supporting a Candidate or Party 95
- Inside America's Campaign Finance Scandals 95
- The Influence of Campaign Finance on Political Participation 96

POLITICAL CAMPAIGN STRATEGIES 97
- Media Influence in U.S. Elections 98
- Social Media's Impact 98
- Political Campaigns: Key Do's and Don'ts 99

CHAPTER 6: CHALLENGES AND OPPORTUNITIES IN GOVERNANCE 101

BIPARTISANSHIP AND UNITY IN GOVERNANCE 101
- The Structure of U.S. Government 101
- The Legislative Process in the United States 102
- Ensuring Governance 102

VOTING RIGHTS IN AMERICA 103
- The American Voting Rights Journey 103
- Understanding How U.S. Elections Work 104

VOTER SUPPRESSION: WHO, HOW, AND WHY 105
- Who Isn't Allowed to Vote? 105
- Evolution of Voter Suppression 106
- Strategies Used to Impede Voting 106
- Use and Justification in the US 107
- Impact on Democracy and Citizenship 107
- When Is Voter Suppression Justifiable? 108

THE ROLE OF LOBBYING AND SPECIAL INTERESTS 108
   What Is Lobbying? *108*
   Lobbying in Political Processes *109*
   Influential Lobbying Groups *109*
   Transparency and Regulation *110*
THE ROLE OF THE JUDICIARY IN DEMOCRACY 110
   Stare Decisis, Activism, and Restraint *111*
   Judicial Structure in the United States *111*
   Constitutional Provisions *113*
GOVERNANCE AND ENVIRONMENTAL SUSTAINABILITY 113
   US Environmental Challenges and Responses *113*
   Environmental Goals vs. Economic Realities *114*
THE ART OF POLITICAL COMPROMISE..114
   Empowering Democracy: Citizen Engagement for Progress *115*
   The Political Balancing Act *115*
THE FUTURE OF AMERICAN DEMOCRACY 116
   Environmental Challenges *116*
   Immigration *117*
   Globalization and Global Order *117*
   Cultural Integration/ Differentiation *117*
   Inequalities *117*
   Disinformation and Misinformation *118*
   Technological Advances and New Ethics Debates *118*
   Political Polarization *118*
   Citizens' Indifference and Lack of Participation *119*

CHAPTER 7: THE POWER OF POLITICAL ENGAGEMENT 121

POLITICAL MOVEMENTS AND CONTEMPORARY DEMOCRACY 121
   Political Movements *121*
YOUTH MOVEMENTS AND POLITICAL CHANGE 123
   Historical Youth Movements *123*
   Current Youth Movements *123*
   U.S. Political Responses to Youth Activism *124*
THE ART OF CIVIL DISCOURSE 125
COMMUNITY ORGANIZING AND GRASSROOTS CAMPAIGNS 126
   The Tale of Accountability and Civic Engagement..*126*
   Tension and Cooperation Between Community Organizing and
   Government..*128*
   The Influence of Grassroots Movements in American Society.........................*129*
DIGITAL ACTIVISM AND SOCIAL MEDIA INFLUENCE 130
   Social Media: Benefits and Challenges *130*
   Social Media's Political Impact in the US *130*
   Social Media Censorship: Legal Battles and Free Speech *131*

NAVIGATING THE POLITICAL LANDSCAPE 132
    What Steps Can Emma Take to Influence the Political Decisions
    That Affect Her Life? 133
THE POWER OF ONE VOTE 133
    My Vote Won't Decide Anything 134
    It is Just One Vote. Nobody Cares 135
    I Don't Like Any of the Candidates 135
    The Power of Voting in Democracy 135
    The Responsibility of Democratic Citizenship 136

CHAPTER 8: NAVIGATING POLITICAL DISCOURSE AND MEDIA 137

THE ERA OF FAKE NEWS AND MISINFORMATION 137
    Influence of Mass Media on Politics: Tactics and Strategies 138
    Democracy's Double-Edged Sword 138
    Fake News and Political Influence 138
    Threats to Democracy 139
MEDIA LITERACY AND CRITICAL THINKING 140
    Traditional Media and Fulfillment of Requirements 140
    Diverse Perspectives in the Digital Era 141
    Journalism's Impartiality Challenge 141
THE POWER OF INVESTIGATIVE JOURNALISM 142
    Real-Life Examples 143
THE INFLUENCE OF POLITICAL SATIRE 143
    Satire Through Time 144
    The Power and Perils of Political Satire 144
THE FUTURE OF POLITICAL COMMUNICATION 145
    Misinformation and Disinformation 145
    Fake News 146
    Virtual Spaces for Political Participation 147
    AI in Politics 148
    Digital Interaction and Democratic Communication 148

CHAPTER 9: AMERICA AND THE WORLD STAGE: BE A GOOD NEIGHBOR 151

AMERICAN POLITICS' GLOBAL IMPACT 151
    Key Milestones: The United States' Impact on Global History 152
    From Cold War to Superpower 152
    American Influence in a Post-Cold War World 153
    Challenges and Benefits of American Hegemony 153
    Global Progress and Challenges 154
THE INFLUENCE OF AMERICAN POLITICS ON GLOBAL GOVERNANCE 155
    Wilson's 14 Points and the Peace of Versailles 155
    Rise of American Hegemony 156
    Key Cold War Moments: Kennedy in Berlin and the Cuban Missile Crisis .. 157
    Cold War Legacy and Modern Geopolitics 158

THE INFLUENCE OF AMERICAN FOREIGN POLICY ON GLOBAL TRADE 159
THE ROLE OF THE AMERICAN GOVERNMENT ON WORLD AFFAIRS 160
   Nuclear Disarmament 161
   Treaty of Paris and Environmental Challenges 161
   Military Intervention 161
   Immigration Policies 161
   International Funding 162
   Strategies for Defending Democracy and Promoting Progress 162

CHAPTER 10: VOICES OF CHANGE AND RESILIENCE 165

ACTIVISM THROUGH ART AND CULTURE 165
   Examples 166
THE LEGACY OF CIVIL RIGHTS MOVEMENTS 167
   Key Figures 167
   Achievements 167
   Ongoing Challenges 168
   Government and Political Responses 168
IMMIGRANT NARRATIVES AND POLITICAL ADVOCACY 169
   Legal Settlement 169
   Accommodation and Housing Facilities 169
   Access to Health and Education 169
   Labor Market 170
   Integration/Discrimination 170
   Political Campaigns and Proposals 170
   Civil Discourse Changes 170
RESILIENCE IN THE FACE OF ADVERSITY 171
   Resilience in Political and Social Crises 171
   Building a Resilient Society 172
   Empowering Citizen Participation for Future Resilience 172

CHAPTER 11: THE AMERICAN DREAM: VOTE IN YOUR OWN BEST INTEREST 175

YOUNG VOTERS' PERSPECTIVES 175
FIRST TIME VOTING 176
   What is Needed? 176
   Election Day 177
POLITICAL AWAKENING 178
POLITICAL JOURNEY: A PERSONAL REFLECTION 179

CONCLUSION 181

REFERENCES 183

Introduction

It always has been, and will continue to be, my earnest desire to learn and to comply, as far as is consistent, with the public sentiment; but it is on great occasions only, and after time has been given for cool and deliberate reflection, that the real voice of the people can be known. —George Washington

This quote was part of a historical correspondence dated May 1, 1796, written by George Washington, who extensively elaborated on the significance of public opinion within the intricate political landscape surrounding the Jay Treaty negotiation between the United States of America and Britain. Within this carefully articulated letter addressed to Edward Carrington, Washington, a statesman from Virginia at the time, adeptly conveyed the necessity of understanding and maneuvering through the nuances of popular sentiment in order to effectively navigate the delicate intricacies of diplomatic relations and national interests during this pivotal period in American history.

During the American Revolution, which took place from 1775 to 1783, George Washington played a pivotal role as the commander-in-chief of the Continental Army. Despite facing a British army with more experience and better resources, Washington's exceptional leadership skills and strategic acumen were instrumental in leading American forces to victory. His ability to inspire and unite troops, coupled with his tactical innovations on the battlefield, ultimately secured the success of the American Revolution.

Following the war, Washington's prestige and leadership qualities led him to be unanimously elected as the first President of the United States in 1789. He served two terms, establishing key precedents for the presidency and helping to shape the young nation's government. This period witnessed the crystallization of American politics. Its seeds of American politics were sown during the colonial period and germinated during the American Revolution.

Early on, political factions began to take shape, paving the way for establishing the enduring two-party system that remains prevalent today. As these factions crystallized, the Federalists, under the leadership of Alexander Hamilton, coalesced into the Federalist Party, while the Anti-Federalists, guided by Thomas Jefferson, transformed into the Democratic-Republican Party. Over time, pivotal issues such as slavery, states' rights, and the extent of governmental authority emerged as critical points of contention, persisting to drive heated debates and influencing the trajectory of American political parties and ideologies. The interplay of these disparate viewpoints and philosophies continues to define the ever-evolving landscape of American politics, shaping the diverse spectrum of beliefs and values that characterize the nation's political discourse.

American politics wasn't born in a single moment; it emerged from a long process of colonial self-governance, revolutionary ideals, and debates about the nature of government. This ongoing conversation and struggle to define the nation's political character continues to shape American politics today.

Democracy, which translates to "rule of the people," took root in ancient Athens approximately 2,500 years ago, flourishing around 500 BC. In stark contrast to prevailing political systems, Athenian democracy empowered its eligible populace—adult, freeborn males—to engage directly in governance via assemblies and judicial proceedings, setting a precedent for citizen involvement in decision-making that would endure through history.

Plato, a renowned Athenian philosopher known for his complex views on governance and society, harbored deep reservations about the practical application of pure democracy because of his belief that the uninformed masses were susceptible to making flawed decisions based on emotions rather than reason and knowledge. In his vision of an ideal republic, Plato emphasized the crucial role of philosophers and guardians who were meticulously trained in the tenets of reason and justice to oversee the governance of the state. Central to Plato's philosophy was the concept that a harmonious and prosperous society could only be realized through a meticulous alignment of individuals fulfilling their designated roles to contribute meaningfully to the collective good. Drawing a parallel between a functioning body and a well-structured state, Plato underscored the significance of every citizen performing their specific duties diligently, whether it involved governance, defense, or the execution of essential functions, thus forming the essential foundation for a flourishing and stable society.

Aristotle, an Athenian philosopher known for his more favorable stance towards democracy compared to some of his peers, viewed democracy not only as a platform for citizen engagement in discussions and decision-making but also as a governing system reliant on the knowledge and wisdom of its populace. Stressing the pivotal role of education in upholding a functional democracy, Aristotle underscored the necessity of a well-informed citizen body. Aligning with Plato's perspective on the pursuit of the good, Aristotle contended that fulfilling one's civic duties was integral to realizing ideal governance. Furthermore, he held firm to the belief that active involvement in civic affairs was not only a civic obligation but also a fundamental element contributing to personal and social welfare.

The concept of politics and good governance has journeyed far. From the Roman Republic's shift from monarchy to a system with elected representatives, the seed of popular participation was sown. John Locke, a champion of liberalism, challenged absolute power with his "Social Contract Theory," emphasizing that governments derive their authority from the consent of the governed. This solidified the concept of popular sovereignty.

The Enlightenment thinkers (a political movement), like Rousseau and Montesquieu, further fueled the fire. Rousseau's book *Social Contract* argued for a government based on the "general will" of the people, while Montesquieu championed the separation of powers to prevent tyranny. These ideas became cornerstones of modern democracies.

From the idea of citizens electing leaders (Rome) to challenging absolute rulers (Locke) and separating government powers (Montesquieu), democracies have grown. Today, more people can vote and choose representatives. But challenges remain, and discussions about improving elections and citizen involvement continue. Through it all, the core idea is that the people hold the ultimate power.

Democracy thrives when its citizens are involved. To jump in, you can become a newshound, staying curious about current affairs and forming your own informed opinions. Sharing your thoughts—responsibly on social media, writing to editors, or attending town halls—lets your representatives hear your voice. Social and political activism takes many forms, from volunteering for campaigns you believe in, to organizing peaceful protests, or joining advocacy groups. These actions raise awareness and push for change. Finally, voting is the ultimate democratic play.

Voting is a crucial element of democratic societies, serving both as a privilege and a responsibility. By voting, citizens express their preferences for how and by whom they are governed, impacting policies that affect everyday life. High voter turnout strengthens the legitimacy and stability of a government, while low turnout can cast doubt on its representativeness.

Voting is not just a right but also a civic duty, essential for sustaining democracy and ensuring it responds to the people's needs. Being informed is vital, as an educated electorate promotes accountable governance and policies that reflect diverse societal interests. Voters should be cognizant of candidates' policies, track records, and governing potential.

The outcomes of elections influence both immediate and long-term decisions on key issues like education, healthcare, and economic policy. Voting also serves as a check on power, allowing citizens to change leaders if they are unsatisfied, thus maintaining a balanced government.

Moreover, voting is a powerful equalizer; every citizen's vote should carry equal weight, regardless of socioeconomic status. Engaged voters are likely to participate more broadly in community life, enhancing democracy and community strength.

This is a journey through American political thought. You'll explore how the main ideas and movements that shaped US politics arose and changed throughout history. Understanding this evolution is key to deciphering the political messages shaping today's socio-political landscape. By seeing how these ideas developed, you'll gain a deeper understanding of where we stand now. This exploration of American political thought is your gateway to a deeper understanding of current affairs. We'll delve into the evolution of the main ideas and movements that have shaped the US, giving you the historical context to decipher today's political landscape. But this journey isn't just about the past—it's about you.

This knowledge empowers you to reflect on society, current events, and the social and political issues we face. It's an invitation to become an active participant in shaping a better tomorrow. Remember, we're all part of a larger whole, and each of us has a role to play in creating a fairer society. So, embark on this journey, and discover how you can make a positive contribution.

Chapter 1:

Understanding Political Ideologies

Navigating the complex world of politics can often feel like embarking on a journey through a labyrinth, with its winding paths, myriad viewpoints, and diverse voices that can be both confusing and enlightening. At the crux of the intricate web of competing visions that define political landscapes are political ideologies—elaborate belief systems dictating how a society ought to operate and evolve. This chapter serves as your compass, equipped with essential tools to traverse this intricate terrain and also gain a deeper understanding of the fundamental principles driving each major political movement.

Delving into the historical origins of these ideologies, we explore their evolution through time, shedding light on the forces that have shaped their development and transformation. By dissecting the historical backdrop that underpins these contrasting belief systems and examining how they diverge on key issues, you will acquire the necessary skills to effectively analyze, compare, and contrast them. Armed with this comprehensive understanding and analytical framework, you will be empowered to critically assess the ongoing political debates that shape contemporary society, enabling you to make well-informed judgments and navigate the dynamic landscape of modern politics with clarity and insight.

Liberalism vs. Conservatism

Throughout history, liberalism and conservatism have emerged as the principal pillars influencing political ideologies globally. Despite occasional overlaps in principles, these two factions differ in their fundamental beliefs and strategies concerning societal progress.

Over the centuries, their contrasting viewpoints have played significant roles in shaping the political scene and public discourse.

Liberalism

Liberals are individuals who typically align with the ideology of progress and transformation. They strive for greater individual freedoms and advocate for the pursuit of social equity, emphasizing on maintaining a just and impartial society. This fundamental belief system is reflected in their policy preferences, which often involve initiatives that aim to level the playing field, such as providing social safety nets for those in need and minimizing governmental interference in personal choice and autonomy.

To illustrate, an individual who identifies as liberal may lend support to initiatives such as the implementation of universal healthcare or the legalization of same-sex marriage.

Conservatism

On the other hand, conservatives place immense importance on tradition, stability, and order within society. They highly value established customs and longstanding institutions, viewing them as linchpins that uphold societal structure. As fervent believers in retaining proven social norms, conservatives advocate for policies that stress individual accountability, frugal government expenditures, and robust national defense mechanisms.

A typical conservative may push for tax reductions to spur economic growth, advocate for the loosening of business regulations to promote entrepreneurship, or champion the reinforcement of traditional family principles as essential foundations for a cohesive society.

Real-World Examples

Environment

Liberals, often motivated by a desire to protect the environment for future generations, may push for more rigorous regulations to hold businesses accountable for their impact on the ecosystem. In contrast, conservatives tend to focus on promoting economic growth and job creation, sometimes accepting certain environmental repercussions in favor of boosting prosperity.

Education

Liberals often believe in the importance of allocating additional government resources to public schools to enhance educational opportunities and foster a diverse and inclusive learning environment. On the other hand, conservatives tend to support the concept of school vouchers or charter schools, which provide parents with greater latitude in determining the best educational path for their children, reflecting their values and preferences.

Crime

When it comes to addressing crime, liberals often prioritize rehabilitation and social programs that aim to tackle the underlying issues that contribute to criminal behavior. In contrast, conservatives tend to lean towards advocating for tougher penalties and a stronger law enforcement presence as a means of deterring criminal activities.

Note: When considering political ideologies, it is vital to recognize that they are broad generalizations that do not capture the complexity of individual beliefs. Each ideology exists along a spectrum, and within this spectrum, individuals may find themselves aligning with various aspects of both liberalism and conservatism. As a strategic move to broaden their appeal and attract diverse voter bases, political parties often blend elements from both ideologies in their policies and messaging. This nuanced approach acknowledges the diverse and evolving nature of political attitudes and preferences among the general populace.

Mutual Criticism

Liberalism and conservatism, as two contrasting political ideologies, engage in a dynamic critique of each other based on their divergent foundational values, priorities, and visions for society.

Liberals often criticize conservatives for their reluctance to embrace change or reform in social, economic, and political systems, arguing that such resistance can hinder societal progress and perpetuate injustices. They also take issue with conservative positions on social issues like abortion, LGBTQ+ rights, and immigration, contending that these positions can be overly restrictive and discriminatory. Economically, liberals critique conservative favoritism towards deregulation and tax cuts for the wealthy, suggesting these policies exacerbate economic inequality and reduce support for vital social services. Environmental issues are another major point of contention, with liberals accusing conservatives of aligning too closely with harmful industrial interests and displaying skepticism towards climate science. Additionally, liberals sometimes paint conservatives as harboring authoritarian tendencies that emphasize order and tradition at the expense of democratic norms and freedoms.

Conversely, conservatives levy their critiques against liberalism by highlighting the problems they see with the liberal emphasis on rapid social change, which they argue can lead to instability and unforeseen negative consequences. They advocate for a more measured approach that values traditions and established norms, viewing these as essential for societal stability. From an economic perspective, conservatives contend that liberal policies of high government spending and extensive regulation can inhibit economic growth and entrepreneurship while fostering dependency on state support. They promote free-market solutions as a means to encourage economic prosperity and personal initiative. Furthermore, conservatives often accuse liberals of promoting moral relativism, which they believe erodes societal values and leads to moral decay. They champion the maintenance of traditional moral standards, which they argue are critical to a healthy society. On the issue of national security, conservatives argue that liberal policies can be dangerously naïve, advocating for a robust defense and strict immigration controls to protect the nation's interests, which they believe liberals often compromise in pursuit of idealistic internationalism and human rights.

These critiques inherently stem from differing views on the role of government, the importance of tradition versus progress, the nature of economic management, and the definitions of freedom and justice. Each paradigm uses its foundational beliefs to evaluate and often challenge the effectiveness and morality of the other's approaches.

Origins and Landmarks

Liberalism and conservatism have fundamentally shaped U.S. political thought, each drawing on European intellectual traditions and evolving distinctly within the American context.

Liberalism in America originated from Enlightenment ideals, emphasizing individual liberty, democracy, and free market principles, as evidenced in the Declaration of Independence and the U.S. Constitution, which were influenced by thinkers like John Locke. The ideology evolved significantly during the 1930s with Franklin D. Roosevelt's New Deal, introducing a shift towards greater governmental intervention in the economy to combat the Great Depression, emphasizing social welfare and economic equality. The 1960s further solidified liberalism's commitment to social justice during the Civil Rights Movement, leading to critical legislation such as the Civil Rights Act and the Voting Rights Act. The late 20th century saw the rise of neoliberalism, advocating reduced government intervention and free market policies. The 21st century has seen liberalism champion progressive causes like marriage equality, environmental policy, and healthcare reform, notably under President Barack Obama with the Affordable Care Act.

Conservatism, developed as a reaction to the radicalism of the French Revolution, emphasizes the preservation of tradition, authority, and religion. In the US, it became more defined in the 1950s and 1960s, with figures like William F. Buckley and Russell Kirk advocating for free market capitalism, limited government, and anti-communism. Barry Goldwater's 1964 presidential campaign and Ronald Reagan's presidency in the 1980s marked significant periods where conservative policies such as tax cuts, deregulation, and strong military stances became central, shifting American politics rightward. The 1990s saw the Republican-led Contract with America, which called for welfare reform and balanced budgets. More recently, the conservative landscape was shaped by the Tea Party's fiscal conservatism and Donald Trump's presidency, which emphasized immigration control, America-first trade policies, and a critique of political correctness.

Both liberalism and conservatism continue to adapt and influence U.S. policy-making and political life, reflecting dynamic responses to historical events and societal changes. Franklin D. Roosevelt, Lyndon B. Johnson, and Barack Obama were pivotal in the evolution of liberalism, while Ronald Reagan, Newt Gingrich, and Donald Trump have been instrumental in defining modern conservatism. These movements and leaders illustrate the ongoing impact and adaptability of these ideologies in shaping American political discourse and policy directions.

Progressivism and Social Change

Two fundamental perspectives help explain how societies function, maintain stability, and experience change. These are structural functionalism and conflict theory, each offering a distinct understanding of societal dynamics.

Structural functionalism sees society as a complex system where various parts work together to promote solidarity and stability. This perspective, associated with theorists like Emile Durkheim and Talcott Parsons, suggests that social institutions such as families, schools, and governments exist because they perform essential functions necessary for society's survival. In this view, changes are slow and evolutionary, generally occurring to adapt to new circumstances but fundamentally aiming at restoring stability.

Conflict theory, influenced by Karl Marx and developed further by figures like Max Weber, views society through a lens of competition and strife among different social classes, ethnic groups, gender groups, and other divisions. This theory posits that societal change is driven by conflict rather than consensus, with the potential for sudden and revolutionary changes rather than gradual evolution. It highlights how economic and power disparities create persistent conflicts that can lead to significant societal shifts.

Modern sociological approaches often blend these perspectives, recognizing that while societies strive for equilibrium, they are also arenas of constant change due to ongoing conflicts among different groups. This synthesis is evident in contemporary theories like feminism and race theory, which extend conflict theory by focusing on the struggles of specific marginalized groups and examining how societal norms and structures perpetuate inequalities.

Revolution

A revolution is a significant and swift change in the organization of a society, usually brought about by drastic and, at times, forceful methods. Those who lead revolutions typically aim to upend the current social, political, and economic structures due to their conviction that these systems are inherently flawed or unfair. Their ultimate objective lies in completely dismantling the existing framework and establishing a new one that better reflects their core beliefs or addresses perceived inequalities and wrongdoings within society. By challenging the status quo and promoting transformation, revolutionaries strive to create a more just and equitable system that resonates with their vision for a more ideal society.

Karl Marx's theory of revolution is one of the most influential, advocating for a proletarian revolution where the working class would overthrow the capitalist class, leading to the dissolution of the class structures themselves. Marxists view revolution as an inevitable part of the historical process, resulting from the inherent conflicts within capitalist systems. Other examples of revolutionary thought can be seen in the American, French, and Russian revolutions, each of which profoundly altered the political and social landscapes of their respective societies in a relatively short period.

Progressivism

Progressivism, in stark contrast to more revolutionary ideologies, supports the concept of effecting social change through gradual and reformative methods embedded within the current political and societal structures. With a focus on the steady advancement of fairness, justice, and equality, progressives engage in a deliberate process of enhancing the fabric of society through the implementation of legislative, social, and economic reforms. They aim not to radically dismantle existing systems, but rather to enhance and optimize them from the inside out. This approach fosters a sense of continuity and evolutionary growth, rendering it less disruptive and more acceptable to a broader spectrum of the population, thereby fostering sustainable and enduring progress.

The progressive approach is often linked to various social movements dedicated to advancing causes such as civil rights, gender equality, and environmental protection. These movements advocate for positive social changes through a variety of strategies, including lobbying for policy adjustments and engaging in activism within the democratic system. This approach emphasizes the importance of unity and collaboration among diverse stakeholders to achieve lasting progress. By concentrating on specific issues and policies, rather than aiming for a complete societal overhaul, proponents of this method seek to implement gradual yet impactful transformations that address pressing social concerns and build a more inclusive and equitable society over time.

Revolutionary and Progressive Movements in History

Historical examples of revolutions and progressive movements illustrate different strategies for societal change. The French Revolution, starting in 1789, initiated widespread discontent against monarchy and inequality, leading to significant changes in French society including the overthrow of the monarchy, the establishment of the Republic, and the global spread of ideals like liberty, equality, and fraternity. Similarly, the Bolshevik Revolution of 1917 in Russia, driven by Vladimir Lenin, replaced the Tsarist autocracy with the communist Soviet Union, significantly influencing global politics and Russian society.

The Cuban Revolution, led by Fidel Castro and Che Guevara, ended Fulgencio Batista's dictatorship and established a socialist state, developing sweeping social and economic reforms including land redistribution and improvements in healthcare and education.

In contrast, progressivism often seeks gradual change within existing systems. The Progressive Era in the United States (1890s–1920s) featured reforms addressing problems of industrialization, including regulatory laws and expansions of democratic participation to the women's suffrage movement. The Civil Rights Movement (1950s–1960s) further exemplifies progressivism through its non-violent approach to ending racial segregation and discrimination, achieving significant legal victories like the Civil Rights Act of 1964 and the Voting Rights Act of 1965.

In the UK, the Labour Party's rise in the early 20th century signified a commitment to progressive social reforms, including the creation of the National Health Service and expansion of the welfare state, aiming to better represent and improve conditions for the working class.

These historical movements underscore the varied approaches to achieving societal change, from revolutionary upheavals to progressive reforms, each leaving lasting impacts on their societies.

Arguments in Favor and Against

Revolution and progressivism represent contrasting approaches to societal change. Revolution is seen as a drastic, often necessary response to corrupt or ineffective political systems, capable of quickly transforming power structures and empowering marginalized groups. While historical instances like the American and French revolutions show the potential to reshape societies and foster new national identities, revolutions often entail significant violence, instability, and unpredictable outcomes. Examples include the post-revolutionary chaos in Russia and authoritarian shifts as seen in the Iranian Revolution, where initial revolutionary ideals were ultimately compromised by power-hungry leaders.

In contrast, progressivism advocates for gradual, deliberate change within existing legal frameworks, promoting stability and sustainability. This method allows for a more inclusive process, incorporating diverse viewpoints and maintaining continuity and security. However, the slow pace of progressive reforms can impede timely solutions to critical injustices, and such reforms are susceptible to being watered down through compromises or obstructed by entrenched powers seeking to preserve their status.

Both approaches have distinct merits and drawbacks, highlighting the complex trade-offs between radical overhaul and incremental improvement in the pursuit of social justice and effective governance. Understanding these dynamics helps in evaluating the most appropriate strategies for societal advancement.

Examples

Progressivism in action comprises a diverse array of political movements, legislative revisions, and policy initiatives aimed at tackling inequality and advancing social justice, as well as fostering environmental sustainability, economic prosperity, and societal well-being. An illustrative example of progressive activism can be seen in the Civil Rights Movement that transpired during the 1950s and 1960s in the United States. This pivotal movement successfully confronted and dismantled racial segregation and discriminatory practices against African Americans, culminating in the pivotal enactment of transformative legislation—the Civil Rights Act of 1964 and the Voting Rights Act of 1965. These historic statutes played a seminal role in eradicating racial bias in key societal domains, such as voting rights, employment opportunities, and access to public accommodations, thus marking significant milestones in the pursuit of equality and justice.

Similarly, the fight for marriage equality over the past few decades serves as a testament to ongoing progress, showcasing the relentless efforts of activists who advocated for, and eventually succeeded in, establishing the legal validation of same-sex unions. This historic struggle reached a significant milestone in the United States with the pivotal Supreme Court ruling in Obergefell v. Hodges in 2015, a decision that unequivocally affirmed the rights of individuals in same-sex relationships to marry, thereby dismantling barriers and recognizing love and commitment without discrimination. The journey toward marriage equality exemplifies the power of collective activism and the triumph of inclusivity and equality in society's evolving landscape.

On the legislative front, the Affordable Care Act, commonly referred to as Obamacare, was signed into law in 2010 by President Barack Obama with the primary goal of enhancing accessibility and affordability in healthcare. This landmark legislation introduced crucial provisions such as safeguards for individuals with pre-existing conditions and the extension of healthcare coverage for young adults up to the age of 26 under their parents' plans.

Furthermore, environmental progressivism was notably exemplified through the implementation and subsequent revisions of the Clean Air Act. In particular, the sweeping amendments made in 1970 marked a significant milestone by broadening the scope of the federal government's responsibilities in overseeing emissions regulation and safeguarding air quality, thereby demonstrating a commitment to environmental protection and public health.

More recent progressive ideas have sparked important conversations and initiatives aimed at addressing pressing issues facing the United States. For instance, the Green New Deal, introduced by Representative Alexandria Ocasio-Cortez and Senator Ed Markey in 2019, emerged as a bold and comprehensive strategy.

This proposal aims not only to combat the urgent threats of climate change but also to tackle economic disparities. The Green New Deal outlines a visionary plan to transition the nation towards sustainable and renewable energies, simultaneously fostering job growth and enhancing social welfare programs.

The Rise of Populism

Populism is a political trend based on the sanctification of the popular classes in a country and adopts a political discourse based on hostility to the institutions of its political system and its societal elites. Its parties and movements have multiplied in Western countries, which has raised fears of its effects on the stability of their ruling regimes.

The origins of populism go back to the period between the 1830s and the 1870s when its trend began in Tsarist Russia and the United States. It was originally called an agricultural movement with socialist tendencies that sought to liberate Russian peasants around 1870 and coincided with the organization of protests in rural America directed against banks and railroad companies.

By the middle of the twentieth century, this term took on a national and social character that freed it from association with the socialist orientation, especially in the Latin American region, especially Argentina.

Although experts in political and social sciences say that it is difficult to define what is meant by the term populism because it is a word loaded with different and sometimes contradictory connotations; others believe that it includes every political speech directed at the popular classes in a country, and based on criticism of its political system, its existing institutions, its societal elites, and its media.

Therefore, populist discourse—characterized by extreme simplification of complex societal issues—is usually carried by charismatic politicians looking for direct popular support by challenging the traditional democratic institutions in their country. They manipulate people's emotions and ideas for political ends and consider themselves to be the authentic national voice and representatives of ordinary citizens or whoever they call them. The forgotten classes.

Thus, they are described as having a tendency in political thinking that rejects the idea of societal diversity and believes in the conflict between the people and the elites, and is prone to demagoguery and anarchism, invoking the centrality of the role of "the people"—whose concept differs from one populist movement to another—in political practice, and based on the political exploitation of feelings of anger among the general public. People especially in times of disasters, economic crises, and political unrest.

Different Approaches of Populism

Populism strives to appeal to ordinary people who feel that their concerns are disregarded by established elite groups. The term is versatile and used to describe a variety of political strategies, ideologies, and movements that assert to champion the interests of the common people.

One way to understand populism is by viewing it as a thin-centered ideology that sees society as divided into two antagonistic groups: the pure people and the corrupt elite. This ideology argues that politics should express the general will of the people. For example, Hugo Chavez in Venezuela promoted a form of socialism that he claimed represented the will and interests of the Venezuelan people against the country's corrupt and elitist past. Donald Trump in the United States also utilized this approach, often portraying his politics as a fight against the "establishment" in Washington, purporting to represent the forgotten men and women against a corrupt cadre of insiders.

Populism can also be considered a political strategy that involves rhetoric claiming to speak for the common people against the elites. Leaders using this strategy often employ simple, direct language and connect through mass rallies or modern media. Silvio Berlusconi in Italy used his media empire and personal charisma to present himself as an outsider to the traditional political class, despite being a wealthy media mogul himself.

Additionally, populism taps into cultural and societal narratives such as nationalism, anti-establishment sentiments, or societal fears like economic decline or immigration. Leaders like Marine Le Pen in France focus on nationalism and strict immigration policies, positioning themselves against perceived threats from external and elitist forces like the European Union.

In economic terms, populism may involve promises of direct economic benefit to the masses, criticism of economic inequality, and sometimes anti-globalization sentiments. This can lean towards left-wing policies focusing on social welfare and redistribution, or right-wing policies concentrating on protectionism and supporting national industries. Juan Perón in Argentina, for example, implemented wide-ranging social welfare programs and nationalized key industries, presenting these moves as a triumph for ordinary Argentines against foreign-controlled economic elites.

Historical examples of populist leaders include Huey Long in the United States during the 1930s, who promoted the "Share Our Wealth" program, promising to cap personal fortunes and provide a guaranteed income to all Americans. Andrew Jackson is often cited as one of the earliest populist leaders, advocating for the rights and power of the common man against established political institutions. Viktor Orban in Hungary employs a mix of nationalism and direct appeals to the common Hungarian, often using the EU and migration as scapegoats for various societal issues.

The Core Characteristics of Populism

Populism, as fascinating as it is complex, defies a single definition. Political theorists analyze it through several key characteristics:

1. **The People vs. The Elite:** Populists divide society into two groups: the virtuous people and the corrupt elite.

    - Historical Example: In the 1890s, the U.S. populist movement, led by William Jennings Bryan, pitted the honest farmers and workers against the wealthy bankers and industrialists of Wall Street.

2. **Anti-Institutionalism:** Populists view established institutions like political parties, media, and academia with suspicion, considering them tools of the elite.

    - Historical Example: Venezuelan president Hugo Chávez (1999–2013) frequently criticized traditional media outlets, calling them instruments of the "oligarchy" and used his talk show to connect directly with supporters.

3. **Plebiscitarianism:** Populists favor direct appeals to the people through referendums and charismatic leadership, bypassing traditional checks and balances.

    - Historical Example: Direct democracy was a key feature of ancient Roman populism. Tribunes, like the Gracchi brothers, would bypass the Senate to propose popular legislation directly to the plebeian assemblies.

4. **Us vs. Them:** Populist leaders frame complex issues in simple terms, creating a sense of national unity against external threats or internal disloyalty.

    - Historical Example: During the French Revolution, Maximilien Robespierre used populist rhetoric to depict France as a pure nation under siege by foreign enemies and domestic traitors.

It's important to note that populism can appear on both the left and right wings of the political spectrum. Understanding these characteristics helps us identify populist movements and analyze their potential impact on democratic institutions.

The Evolution of American Populism

Populism in the United States has a rich historical backdrop, dating back to the late 19th century with the rise of the People's Party. Rooted in economic disparity and social disenfranchisement, populist movements advocate for the interests of ordinary citizens against perceived elite domination. Over time, factors such as economic inequality, globalization, cultural shifts, political polarization, and media fragmentation have fueled the resurgence of populism in the latter half of the 20th century and into the 21st. Economic insecurities stemming from stagnant wages and job loss, coupled with anxieties over cultural changes and political gridlock, have created fertile ground for populist rhetoric. Moreover, the advent of digital media has facilitated the dissemination of populist messages, allowing leaders to bypass traditional gatekeepers and connect directly with their base. This confluence of factors has propelled populist figures into the spotlight, reshaping the political landscape and challenging established norms. As populism continues to influence American politics, its long-term impact remains a subject of debate, underscoring the enduring relevance of this historical phenomenon.

Feminism and Gender Politics

The Evolution of Feminist Movements

The feminist movement, viewed through a sociological lens, encompasses a broad range of ideologies, goals, and strategies aimed at achieving gender equality and challenging patriarchal structures in society. At its core, feminism seeks to address social, political, and economic inequalities experienced by women, as well as other marginalized genders, such as non-binary and transgender individuals.

From a historical perspective, feminism has evolved through different waves, each responding to the specific social and political contexts of its time. The first wave of feminism emerged in the 19th and early 20th centuries, focusing primarily on securing legal rights for women, such as suffrage and property rights. This wave was characterized by activism centered around issues like women's education, workplace rights, and reproductive autonomy.

The second wave, which gained momentum in the 1960s and 1970s, broadened the feminist agenda to include a wider range of issues, such as reproductive rights, equal pay, and combating gender-based violence. This wave also critiqued traditional gender roles and norms, advocating for women's liberation and autonomy in all aspects of life.

The third wave of feminism, emerging in the 1990s and continuing into the 21st century, emphasized intersectionality and diversity within the movement. Intersectional feminism acknowledges that gender intersects with other social categories such as race, class, sexuality, and disability, shaping individuals' experiences of oppression and privilege. This wave also focused on amplifying the voices of marginalized communities within feminism, including women of color, LGBTQ+ individuals, and people with disabilities.

From a political perspective, feminism has influenced policy-making at local, national, and international levels. Feminist activists and organizations have successfully lobbied for legislative changes to address issues like domestic violence, sexual harassment, and workplace discrimination. Additionally, feminist movements have been instrumental in shaping public discourse and challenging cultural norms that perpetuate gender inequality.

Feminism isn't a movement against men or their rights; rather, it's focused on achieving real equal opportunities and rights for women. It seeks to dismantle gender-based discrimination and create a society where individuals of all genders can thrive. Feminism challenges societal norms and structures that limit women's potential and perpetuate inequality. By advocating for gender equality, feminism benefits everyone by promoting fairness, justice, and inclusivity in all aspects of life.

Overall, the feminist movement is a dynamic and multifaceted social phenomenon that continues to evolve in response to changing social, political, and economic conditions. While progress has been made in many areas, challenges such as systemic sexism, gender-based violence, and reproductive injustice persist, highlighting the ongoing need for feminist activism and advocacy.

Patriarchy

Patriarchy is a social system where men hold primary power and dominate in various aspects of life, including politics, economics, and culture, while women are often relegated to subordinate roles. This system has deep historical roots in Western civilization, dating back to ancient times, when male dominance was prevalent in family structures, politics, and religious institutions.

Throughout history, patriarchy has been sustained through religious teachings, legal systems, and cultural norms, perpetuating gender inequality and denying women equal rights and opportunities. Women have faced discrimination and marginalization, restricted in their ability to participate fully in society.

In response to these injustices, the feminist movement emerged in the 19th century, advocating for women's suffrage, legal rights, and social equality. Feminists challenged patriarchal norms, seeking to dismantle gender roles and stereotypes that limited individuals based on their gender. They fought for equality in all aspects of life, aiming to end discrimination and empower women and marginalized genders.

The feminist movement recognizes the intersectionality of oppression, understanding that patriarchy intersects with other forms of discrimination, such as racism and classism. By addressing these intersections, feminism aims to create a more inclusive and equitable society for all.

Feminism poses a significant challenge to patriarchy by advocating for gender equality, challenging traditional gender roles, and promoting social justice. Through activism, advocacy, and education, feminists continue to work towards a society where all genders have equal rights, opportunities, and representation, free from the constraints of patriarchy.

From Suffragettes to Contemporary Advocacy

The feminist movement has evolved through several waves, each addressing different aspects of gender inequality and discrimination. One of the earliest and most impactful phases was the suffragette movement, which began in the late 19th and early 20th centuries. Suffragettes fought vehemently for women's right to vote, enduring significant opposition and persecution. Their activism included protests, hunger strikes, and civil disobedience.

The suffragettes achieved a monumental victory with the passage of the 19th Amendment to the United States Constitution in 1920, which granted women the right to vote. This milestone marked a significant step forward in the fight for gender equality and paved the way for subsequent feminist movements.

The second wave of feminism emerged in the 1960s and 1970s, addressing a wide range of issues, including reproductive rights, workplace discrimination, and gender roles. Feminists advocated for access to contraception and abortion, equal pay for equal work, and an end to gender-based discrimination in employment and education.

Key achievements of the second wave include the passage of Title IX in 1972, prohibiting sex discrimination in federally funded educational programs, and the legalization of abortion in the landmark Supreme Court case Roe v. Wade in 1973.

In contemporary times, feminists continue to advocate for various rights and issues affecting women in the United States. These include reproductive rights, workplace equality, ending gender-based violence, LGBTQ+ rights, and embracing intersectional feminism to address the unique experiences of marginalized groups.

Gender Gap

The World Economic Forum's Global Gender Gap Report paints a clear picture: globally, women have less economic opportunity (only 40% employed compared to 50% of men), hold fewer leadership positions (27%), and are underrepresented in STEM fields (35% of graduates). While there's near parity in basic education enrollment, health disparities and a lack of political representation (26% of parliamentary seats, 11% of heads of state) persist.

The situation in the United States isn't much better. Women's labor force participation (47%) has stalled, and they earn significantly less than men (82 cents per dollar). Leadership positions across sectors remain male-dominated, with women holding less than 30% in key areas like Congress and Fortune 500 companies. Although women outnumber men in college degrees, they are still underrepresented in STEM fields.

These statistics offer undeniable evidence of a global gender gap, with the United States mirroring many of the same inequalities.

Gender Policies

Gender politics refers to how power dynamics and societal norms intersect with gender to influence political discourse and policies. To bridge the gender gap, gender politics must translate into effective gender policies. Gender policies should prioritize equal representation by increasing the presence of women and marginalized genders in all sectors through affirmative action and diversity initiatives. Additionally, policies must address economic disparities by ensuring equal pay for equal work and providing opportunities for education and entrepreneurship.

Healthcare policies should guarantee access to comprehensive services, including reproductive healthcare, and address gender-based violence by implementing laws to hold perpetrators accountable and support survivors. In education, policies should eliminate gender stereotypes, provide equal opportunities in STEM fields, and combat discrimination and harassment.

An intersectional approach is crucial, acknowledging the intersecting oppressions faced by individuals based on race, ethnicity, class, sexuality, and ability. By addressing these intersections, policies can better meet the diverse needs and experiences of marginalized communities. Overall, effective gender policies translate gender politics into actionable measures that promote equality and inclusivity, ultimately bridging the gender gap and creating a more equitable society for all genders.

Driving Change: Feminist Strategies in Contemporary Politics

In the contemporary political landscape, the feminist movement remains actively engaged in advocating for gender equality and pushing for policies that address issues affecting women and marginalized genders. Through various means of participation, feminists work to influence the political system and advance their goals:

Feminist organizations and activists engage in advocacy efforts to raise awareness about gender inequality and lobby lawmakers for legislative and policy changes. They focus on issues such as reproductive rights, equal pay, healthcare access, and ending gender-based violence.

In electoral politics, feminists aim to increase the representation of women and marginalized genders in political office. They support feminist candidates, mobilize voters, and work to elect leaders who prioritize gender-inclusive policies.

Community organizing is another key strategy employed by feminists, as they mobilize support for gender equality initiatives at the local level. Through grassroots organizations, workshops, and coalition-building efforts, they empower individuals to advocate for change in their communities.

Feminist activists also utilize protest and direct action to draw attention to pressing gender issues and demand policy reforms. These actions raise public awareness and pressure policymakers to address issues such as reproductive rights, gender-based violence, and workplace discrimination.

Additionally, feminist legal organizations provide legal support to individuals facing discrimination or injustice based on gender. They litigate cases, file amicus briefs, and work to shape legal precedents that protect women's rights and advance gender justice.

Overall, the feminist movement employs a range of strategies, including advocacy, electoral politics, community organizing, protest, and legal advocacy, to influence the political system and create a more equitable society for all genders.

Conservative Critiques of Feminism

Critics from conservative sectors of society present various arguments against feminism and gender politics, reflecting ideological differences and concerns about traditional values, societal stability, and gender roles.

Firstly, they argue that feminism undermines traditional gender roles and family structures, which they believe are essential for societal stability and morality. Critics claim that feminism promotes non-traditional lifestyles and values that threaten the traditional family unit.

Secondly, some conservatives assert that feminism emasculates men and challenges traditional notions of masculinity. They argue that feminist ideologies seek to diminish male authority and dominance in society, posing a threat to men's identity and social status.

Critics also argue that feminism promotes moral relativism and cultural decay by challenging traditional values and norms. They contend that feminist ideologies undermine religious teachings and cultural traditions, leading to societal instability and moral decline.

Additionally, conservatives assert that feminism seeks special treatment for women at the expense of men's rights and opportunities. Policies such as affirmative action and gender quotas are seen as unfairly advantaging women and discriminating against men.

Critics further argue that feminism disrupts the natural social order by challenging hierarchical structures and power dynamics. They believe that gender equality threatens social stability and cohesion by challenging traditional hierarchies and redistributing power in society.

Some critics also assert that feminism fosters anti-men sentiment and fosters divisiveness between genders. They claim that feminist rhetoric demonizes men and portrays them as oppressors, leading to hostility and resentment between men and women.

Lastly, opponents criticize what they perceive as excessive political correctness and censorship in feminist discourse. They argue that feminists suppress dissenting opinions and stifle free speech in the name of gender equality.

Overall, conservative opposition to feminism and gender politics stems from concerns about traditional values, societal stability, masculinity, moral decay, and perceived threats to men's rights and social status. These arguments reflect deeper ideological divides over gender roles, social norms, and the role of government in promoting equality and social justice.

Chapter 2:

Unraveling the Political Parties System

In this chapter, we explore the vital role political parties play in governance, acting as the threads that connect ideologies, policies, and power dynamics. We delve into their historical roots, evolving philosophies, and contemporary significance.

Starting from the inception of democracy to today's electoral battlegrounds, we trace the origins and development of major political parties, highlighting pivotal moments that shaped their trajectory. By examining the historical context, we uncover the ideological foundations and strategic maneuvers of each party, from liberal ideals to conservative traditions.

Additionally, the chapter offers a framework for comparing political ideologies, guiding readers through the diverse landscape of party platforms, policies, and priorities. Through this analysis, readers gain insights into the nuanced differences and underlying principles that shape each party's vision for society.

Understanding Political Parties

Political Parties vs. Social Organizations

Political parties are organized groups of individuals with shared ideologies and goals, aiming to gain political power and influence government policies. They contest elections, seek to hold office, and implement their agenda once in power. Their structure is hierarchical, with leadership, membership, and formal decision-making processes, often spanning local, regional, and national levels.

In contrast to political parties, other social organizations, such as charities, NGOs, and advocacy groups, focus on specific social issues, providing services, or advocating for particular causes without seeking political power. They vary in structure, from hierarchical to decentralized networks, and engage in activities like humanitarian aid, environmental protection, human rights, and healthcare.

Political parties have a broad membership base and seek support from diverse segments of society. They appeal to voters across demographics and socio-economic backgrounds, aiming to secure electoral victories. In contrast, other social organizations have specialized membership bases, comprising individuals passionate about specific causes or issues.

Political parties are accountable to their members, supporters, and the electorate, governed by electoral laws and regulations. They endure beyond individual leaders or specific issues, maintaining continuity in their organizational structure and core ideologies. Other social organizations are also accountable but to donors, stakeholders, and the communities they serve rather than the general public. They may have a more fluid existence, emerging in response to specific needs or crises and disbanding once their objectives are achieved.

While political parties engage in various activities, such as campaigning, policy formulation, and governance, other social organizations focus on specific areas like humanitarian aid, environmental protection, human rights, and education. They may collaborate with political parties on specific issues but maintain autonomy from them.

Overall, political parties play a central role in democratic governance, providing a mechanism for citizens to participate in the political process. Other social organizations contribute to civil society through diverse activities and advocacy efforts, addressing specific social issues and providing services to communities. Both types of organizations are essential for a healthy and vibrant society, each fulfilling distinct roles in shaping public discourse and advancing social change.

In the table below, we find the key differences:

	Political Party	Social Organization
Purpose	To gain power and shape government policies through elections and governance.	To address specific social issues, provide services, or advocate for particular causes without seeking political power.
Structure	Hierarchical structures with leadership, membership, and formal decision-making processes spanning local, regional, and national levels.	Vary in structure, ranging from hierarchical to decentralized networks, depending on their objectives and the nature of their work.
Duration	Endure beyond individual leaders or specific issues, maintaining continuity in their organizational structure and core ideologies.	Vary widely, as they may emerge in response to specific needs or crises and disband once their objectives are achieved or circumstances change.
Activities	Various activities such as campaigning, policy formulation, and governance to secure electoral victories and influence government decisions.	Various activities such as humanitarian aid, environmental protection, human rights advocacy, and healthcare provision to address specific social issues and serve communities.

The Crucial Role of Political Parties in Modern Democracies

Political parties are integral to the functioning of contemporary political systems, especially those grounded in republican and democratic principles. They play a multifaceted role that enhances political organization, public policy formulation, government stability, leadership development, representation, accountability, public participation, and the mediation of public opinion.

Political parties help structure the political space by offering voters clear, organized choices during elections. They consolidate complex political, social, and economic ideas into more comprehensible platforms, simplifying decision-making for voters. This structure not only aids in the electoral process but also in framing public debate and clarifying where parties stand on critical issues, thereby influencing both public opinion and policy priorities.

At the heart of their function, parties are crucial to the development and advocacy of public policies. Party platforms, which outline proposed laws and solutions to societal issues, are fundamental in shaping the national agenda. These platforms are often developed through internal deliberations, expert consultations, and public feedback, reflecting a comprehensive approach to addressing national concerns. By promoting these platforms, parties not only inform the electorate but also commit to future governance strategies that are crucial during their campaigns for office.

Once in power, whether through securing a majority or forming coalitions, parties are vital in organizing government operations. They appoint party members to key governmental and administrative positions, thereby ensuring that the executive and legislative branches are capable of enacting and sustaining their proposed policies. This organization is essential for maintaining governmental stability and continuity—attributes that are particularly important in times of crisis or when navigating complex international and domestic challenges.

Political parties are also central to the recruitment and nurturing of political leaders. Through their ranks, parties identify potential leaders, providing them with the necessary exposure, experience, and resources to advance politically. This approach not only ensures a steady influx of leadership but also promotes a cadre of officials who are well-versed in party philosophy, governance practices, and legislative procedures.

Beyond organizing government and nurturing leaders, parties serve as a vital link between the government and the populace. They represent diverse societal interests, advocating for policies that reflect the aspirations and needs of different groups. This representation is fundamental in democratic societies, where legitimizing government action requires broad public support and participation. Through parties, citizens can see their interests reflected in national policies, enhancing both the inclusivity and legitimacy of the governing process.

Accountability is another critical role played by political parties. When in power, parties strive to implement their agendas and are held accountable by the electorate for their governance. Conversely, opposition parties scrutinize the actions of the ruling party, critiquing their policies and governance to keep them in check. This dynamic ensures a healthy democratic process, fostering transparency and accountability while encouraging a competitive yet constructive political environment.

Furthermore, political parties are key in mobilizing voter participation. They engage with citizens through campaigns, debates, and grassroots community activities, energizing the electorate and encouraging broader civic participation. This engagement is crucial for the health of a democracy, as it fosters an informed, active, and engaged citizenry.

Lastly, political parties play a significant role in shaping and channeling public opinion. They not only respond to the evolving concerns and preferences of the public but also have the power to influence and guide public opinion on various issues. Through ongoing dialogue with constituents, media engagement, and public campaigning, parties reflect and sometimes shape societal values and priorities.

In conclusion, political parties are foundational to the effective functioning of democratic and republican political systems. They provide necessary organization, foster leadership, ensure representation and accountability, and stimulate political participation and public debate.

Without political parties, modern political systems would struggle to maintain stability, responsiveness, and democratic engagement, underscoring their critical role in both governing and in the broader societal context.

Understanding Political Party Systems

Political party systems come in a spectrum, reflecting how many parties compete for power and the level of competition allowed.

At one end lies the **two-party system**, where dominant parties like the U.S. Democrats and Republicans hold center stage. Third parties rarely challenge their grip, making elections a two-horse race.

In a **multiparty system**, the doors open wider. Three or more parties have a shot at winning and influencing policy. Often, governing requires coalitions, alliances between multiple parties, as seen in India with its Bharatiya Janata Party (BJP) and Indian National Congress alongside various regional parties. Germany's Christian Democrats, Social Democrats, Greens, and Liberals offer another example.

Things get concerning with less democratic systems that lack genuine competition and often restrict political freedoms. A **dominant-party system**, like China's with the Communist Party, maintains control through various means, limiting opposition or manipulating elections. Other parties might exist, but they're on the sidelines. Another example of this system is the Syrian system with the Al-Baath party.

The most extreme is the **one-party system**, a one-man show where only one party is legal, like North Korea's Workers' Party. Opposition parties are banned, and any dissent is squashed.

The type of system a country has significantly impacts its government and the level of democracy it enjoys. Two-party systems can offer stability and clear choices, but they can also limit options and stifle new ideas. Multiparty systems can be more representative but can also lead to complex governments and instability. And less democratic systems often lack accountability and restrict citizen participation, raising concerns about fairness and representation.

Determining the type of party system in a political landscape involves assessing several key indicators. Firstly, the number of dominant parties plays a crucial role. A two-party system is characterized by two major parties dominating the political arena, while a multiparty system features several influential parties. Conversely, a one-party system is

36

marked by the dominance of a single party, and a dominant-party system may have multiple parties, but one consistently holds power.

Examining election outcomes is essential for understanding power distribution. In a two-party system, one of the two major parties typically secures a majority of seats or victories. In multiparty systems, no single party usually achieves an outright majority, often leading to coalition governments. Conversely, in one-party systems, the ruling party consistently dominates elections.

Voter behavior is another critical indicator. In two-party systems, voters often exhibit strong loyalty to one of the two major parties. In multiparty systems, voter support may be divided among various parties, leading to diverse electoral outcomes. In one-party systems, voter choices may be limited by the dominance of the ruling party.

Additionally, observing legislative functioning provides insights into party dynamics. In two-party systems, legislative debates are often polarized between the two major parties. In multiparty systems, coalition-building and negotiation are common for passing legislation. In one-party systems, legislative bodies may predominantly serve the interests of the ruling party.

Here's a breakdown of the advantages and disadvantages of different political party systems considering different aspects:

	Two-party system	Multiparty system	Dominant-party system	One-party system
Alternation in Power	Limited.	More frequent; change is allowed.	Unlikely; discourages opposition.	Impossible.
Social Change	Slow.	Faster and more responsive.	Controlled by the dominant party.	Suppressed.
Stability	Clear lines	Lower due to	High, but	Absolute.

	of authority. Strong majority can lead to decisive action.	coalition negotiations.	mask underlying tensions.	
Citizens' Participation	High due to clear choices.	High due to diverse options.	Limited, discourages opposition.	Extremely limited, no choice.
Progress in All Fields	Steady but may lack innovation.	Multifaceted but may lack focus.	Dictated by the dominant party's interests.	Limited to the party's objectives.
Representation	Limited; may not reflect all societal views and interests.	Better reflects societal makeup.	Limited to the dominant party's ideology.	Nonexistent.
Minority Rights	Vulnerable depending on the majority party.	Protected due to competition.	It may be tolerated but not actively promoted.	Suppressed.

Concentration /Dispersion of Power	Power is concentrated in two parties, which can lead to a lack of competition.	Dispersed among multiple parties; determined by coalitions.	Concentrated in the dominant party.	Absolute concentration in one party.
Threat of Authoritarian Power	High if one party dominates for too long. Over time, this can lead to a decline in accountability and a weakening of democratic institutions.	Lower due to competition between different parties.	High; dominant party usually become authoritarian.	Absolute.
Governability	Efficient due to clear majority.	Complex due to coalition negotiations.	Efficient but lacks responsiveness.	Absolute control.

The Role of Third-Party Candidates

In politics, a third-party system means there are more than two major parties competing for power. These extra parties add variety to the system by representing different viewpoints and people. They can make

39

government more balanced, bring new ideas, and help unheard voices get heard. It's important to understand how these parties work and what effects they can have, both positive and negative.

Third parties engage with government through electoral participation, fielding candidates from local to national levels. Winning seats enables them to influence legislation, proposing bills aligned with their agenda. They actively participate in political discourse, advocating for their policies, and scrutinizing the major parties. By spotlighting overlooked issues, they enrich public debate and challenge the status quo.

Third-Party Importance

For Balance of Power

Third parties challenge the two-party system by offering voters a choice and forcing major parties to consider new ideas. In some cases, they even hold the key to forming a government, making it more representative.

For Progress

Third parties bring fresh ideas. They push for new solutions and challenge the way things are done, keeping politics moving forward.

For Negotiation Processes

Third parties in multiparty governments help make deals. They bring different viewpoints to the table, forcing bigger parties to work together and find common ground. This keeps things running smoothly and represents everyone better.

For Representation of Underrepresented Voices

Third parties give a voice to those often left out. They champion the needs of minority groups, making sure everyone has a say in how things are run.

Third-Party Rise and System Disruption

Various factors spur the emergence of third parties, including dissatisfaction with major parties, neglected issues, charismatic leaders, or social movements. Economic crises and cultural shifts also fuel their rise. While third parties can positively impact politics, they may destabilize the system if not integrated properly. Disruption tactics like obstructionism or extremism and the fragmentation of power among parties can hinder governance, causing gridlock and instability.

Historical Examples of Third-Party Emergence

Throughout American history, third parties have emerged as significant forces. The Anti-Masonic Party, formed in the 1820s due to anti-Mason sentiment, reached its peak in the 1832 election with William Wirt as its candidate. Similarly, the Populist Party, founded in the late 19th century by farmers and laborers, advocated for government intervention in regulating railroads and increasing money supply. Their presidential candidate James B. Weaver in 1892 didn't win, but the party influenced the Democratic Party to adopt some of their policies.

Likewise, the Progressive Party, established by former President Theodore Roosevelt in 1912, addressed concerns about corruption, trusts, and social welfare. Though Roosevelt lost the presidential election running as a Progressive, the party's influence led to the adoption of many progressive reforms. These examples showcase third parties as catalysts for change, raising crucial issues, influencing major parties, and even electing figures who challenge the political status quo, even if they themselves aren't always successful in winning elections.

Representative Third Parties in Modern Political Systems

In Spain, the emergence of Vox in the early 21st century significantly impacted the country's political landscape. As a right-wing populist party, Vox posed a notable challenge to the long-established dominance of the traditional conservative and socialist parties. The party strategically tapped into the escalating nationalist sentiments sweeping across the nation, deftly channeling the growing dissatisfaction felt by many regarding the handling of contentious issues, like immigration and regional autonomy. Despite facing widespread criticism and backlash for its provocative and polarizing stances, Vox managed to successfully secure seats both in regional and national legislative bodies. This has not only solidified Vox's presence in the political arena but also wielded considerable influence over the ongoing discourse and policymaking in Spain.

Ecologist parties, recognizing the urgent need for holistic solutions in today's complex world, have garnered significant attention within diverse political landscapes globally. By placing a strong emphasis on promoting the crucial values of environmental sustainability and social equity, these parties strive to address pressing issues through multifaceted approaches. Their advocacy extends to a wide array of progressive policies, encompassing areas such as the allocation of resources towards renewable energy initiatives, implementation of conservation strategies to protect biodiversity, and the promotion of sustainable development practices. Noteworthy is the strategic alliances formed by ecologist parties in countries like Germany and France, where collaborations with other forward-thinking political groups have effectively shaped environmental agendas at both national and European levels, showcasing the impact of united efforts on policy-making and meaningful change.

In the UK, the Liberal Democrats have historically played a significant role as a third party, effectively challenging the long-standing dominance of the Conservative and Labour parties. However, the emergence of the Scottish National Party (SNP) and the Brexit Party in more recent years has significantly altered the country's political landscape. The SNP's primary agenda of advocating for Scottish independence and the Brexit Party's staunch Eurosceptic stance have introduced a new element of complexity to the traditional two-party system. Consequently, the British political arena now grapples with increased fragmentation and heightened uncertainty as these parties' ideologies and priorities continue to reshape the dynamics and discourse within the realm of UK politics.

Political Party Ideologies

Political parties are more than just groups wearing different colors; they embody unique beliefs and principles regarding the optimal functioning of society. These organizations serve as vehicles for advocating diverse policies and strategies, shaping the future trajectory of governance and public discourse.

Right-Wing Parties

Known for their adherence to conservatism, place a strong emphasis on upholding traditional values such, as family, religion, and patriotism. In addition to advocating for limited government involvement in the economy, they stress the importance of individuals taking responsibility for their own actions. Moreover, these parties prioritize national security and the enforcement of law and order within society, alongside their consistent support for free-market capitalism as an essential economic system.

Left-Wing Parties

Characterized by their alignment with progressive or radical political ideologies, have a core focus on advocating for social equality and economic justice while promoting government intervention to tackle various societal concerns effectively. One of their main priorities lies in implementing policies that center around wealth redistribution mechanisms, including the establishment of robust social welfare programs alongside initiatives aimed at safeguarding and preserving the environment for future generations.

Center Parties

Strategically position themselves as moderate entities, advocating for compromise and pragmatism in their policy approaches. By incorporating facets of both left and right-wing ideologies, they craft a nuanced political agenda that endeavors to strike a harmonious balance and resonate with a diverse array of voters across the political spectrum.

Anarchist Parties

Believe in challenging traditional power dynamics and envision a future where centralized authority is dismantled in favor of collective empowerment. By rejecting established governance models, they rally for grassroots initiatives and autonomous communities shaping the fabric of society through mutual support and consensus-building. In essence, anarchists champion self-governing structures, striving for a harmonious existence built on mutual respect and solidarity among all individuals.

Democrats and Republicans

In the United States, Democrats and Republicans are the two dominant political parties that uphold contrasting ideologies. Democrats tend to espouse left-wing values, championing progressive stances on issues like social welfare, healthcare reform, and environmental conservation. Conversely, Republicans gravitate towards right-wing conservatism, emphasizing the importance of minimal government intervention, promoting free-market economics, and upholding traditional beliefs and values. These differing perspectives shape the political landscape and influence public policy decisions, reflecting the diverse range of opinions and priorities held by Americans across the political spectrum.

Examples

Right-wing parties are found in various countries, such as the Republican Party in the US, which emphasizes smaller government, individual liberty, and fiscal conservatism. In the UK, the Conservative Party focuses on traditional values, limited immigration, and a strong national defense. France's National Rally prioritizes national identity, stricter immigration policies, and law and order. In Italy, La Lega (The League) stands as a right-wing political party known for its emphasis on regional autonomy, anti-immigration stance, and Euroscepticism.

On the left, the Democratic Party in the US supports social welfare programs, environmental protection, and labor unions. The UK's Labour Party champions social justice, universal healthcare, and government intervention in the economy. Germany's Social Democratic Party advocates for strong social safety nets, worker rights, and progressive taxation.

Center parties like Germany's Christian Democratic Union promote a balance between social welfare and economic prosperity with Christian values. France's La République En Marche, focuses on pragmatic solutions, social reforms, and European integration. In Canada, the Liberal Party emphasizes social justice, economic opportunity, and environmental sustainability.

Anarchist ideals are represented by groups rather than traditional political parties. For instance, in Spain, the CNT (Confederación Nacional del Trabajo - National Confederation of Labor) advocates for worker self-management and direct democracy. In Greece, the Anarkhiko Metopo (Anarchist Front) promotes anti-authoritarianism, workers' rights, and environmentalism.

Analyzing Parties in the United States

In the United States, the two major political parties are the Republican Party and the Democratic Party, each embodying distinct ideologies and policy priorities. The Republican Party, rooted in conservative principles, upholds values such as advocating for smaller government to enhance individual liberties and maintaining fiscal conservatism. They champion free-market capitalism, advocate for lower taxes to spur economic growth, and prefer minimal government interference in economic affairs. Furthermore, Republicans place a strong emphasis on national security, law and order, and preserving traditional values. Their platform often includes opposition to abortion rights, staunch support for gun rights, and a critical stance towards environmental regulations.

On the other hand, the Democratic Party represents a more progressive viewpoint, prioritizing social welfare programs, environmental preservation, and the rights of labor unions. Democrats strive to address income inequality by advocating for policies that expand access to healthcare and education while aiming to combat climate change. Additionally, they focus on promoting LGBTQ+ rights, advocating for racial justice, and championing women's rights. Noteworthy elements of the Democratic platform are centered around healthcare reform, proposals to raise the minimum wage, and initiatives to bolster social safety nets.

Chapter 3:

Navigating the Electoral Process

From the very inception of the nation, the electoral process in the United States has stood as a cornerstone of the American identity, playing a pivotal role in shaping the course of history and reflecting the tapestry of its diverse populace throughout time.

Citizens engage in a deep-rooted tradition that embodies democratic values and community involvement. Yet, behind this process lie complex rules and institutions that influence each person's voting journey, highlighting the intricate nature of democracy. We will delve deep into the diverse facets that influence democratic decision-making. By dissecting the functions of political parties, scrutinizing the pivotal roles of primaries and caucuses, and dissecting the nuances of the Electoral College system, we aim to provide a thorough understanding of how these components interplay to determine the course of the American nation's governance.

The Elections

Elections are the cornerstone of a republican system, where they play a pivotal role in ensuring that the government truly represents the collective voice of the populace. In a republic, elected representatives are entrusted with the vital task of making decisions on behalf of the citizens they serve, with these electoral processes providing the platform for voters to effectively select their leaders and hold them answerable for their actions. The fundamental significance of elections is deeply rooted in their function of upholding a government structure that remains both responsive and transparent to its people. Through the mechanism of elections, individuals have the power to not only shape governmental policies through their choices but also to bring about change by replacing leaders who fail to meet their expectations and endorsing those whose aspirations and values resonate with their own.

The periodic nature of elections is crucial because it ensures continuity and change in governance. Regular elections provide a structured opportunity for citizens to reassess and renew their leadership. They prevent stagnation and the entrenchment of power by offering regular intervals at which new ideas and leaders can emerge. The recurrence of elections also acts as a check on the power of incumbents, compelling them to govern more effectively, address the needs of their constituents, and mitigate corruption, as their desire for reelection depends on their performance.

Without periodic elections, a republican system would risk devolving into authoritarianism. Without the regular mandate from voters, leaders could potentially ignore public needs and interests, leading to disenfranchisement and dissatisfaction. The absence of elections would likely lead to increased corruption, fewer checks on power, and possibly social unrest, as the public would lack a formal mechanism to change their rulers or influence government policies. Thus, elections are essential for sustaining democracy, ensuring government legitimacy, and fostering a healthy political environment where citizens' rights and voices are respected and acted upon.

Participating in elections is crucial because it empowers individuals by providing them with the opportunity to actively engage in the democratic process, allowing them to play a significant role in shaping the policies that directly impact their daily lives and future prospects. By casting their votes, individuals can effectively voice their opinions on crucial governance issues, contributing to the discourse on public matters and advocating for the changes they wish to see in society. Furthermore, the act of voting serves as a vital mechanism for holding leaders accountable, as it compels elected officials to prioritize the interests and concerns of the public they serve. Encouraging high voter turnout not only reinforces the legitimacy of the democratic system but also fosters a government that is truly representative of the diverse wills and aspirations of its citizens. Ultimately, each ballot cast serves as a fundamental building block in fortifying the health and resilience of democracy, perpetuating a system where every voice counts and every vote matters in shaping the collective future of a nation.

Globally, political systems utilize diverse election methods, each shaping the democratic process uniquely. The first-past-the-post (FPTP) system, common in the US and UK, awards victory to the candidate with the most votes in a district, often benefiting larger parties and potentially resulting in a disproportionate allocation of seats relative to the total vote share. In contrast, proportional representation (PR), used in many European countries, allocates seats based on the percentage of votes each party receives, fostering greater diversity in parliaments but sometimes leading to coalition governments.

Additionally, some countries adopt mixed electoral systems, like Germany's mixed-member proportional representation, which combines direct candidate votes with party list votes to balance direct constituency representation with broader proportional fairness. Systems like the single transferable vote and ranked-choice voting allow voters to rank candidates by preference, aiming to ensure that elected officials represent a true majority.

These electoral systems reflect various priorities and theories on the best ways to represent the will of the people, thus affecting the overall health and functionality of democracies worldwide.

Eligibility for U.S. Elections

In the United States, distinct criteria apply to individuals wishing to vote or run for office, as outlined by federal and state laws.

Voter Eligibility

To participate in federal and state elections by casting a vote, an essential prerequisite is citizenship. Each voter is required to be a resident of the state where they choose to register, and they must meet precise age criteria, typically at least 18 years old by the date of Election Day. The enrollment process is compulsory and comes with specific deadlines that can differ by state. It should be noted that one's legal status could impact their voting privileges, as in some states, individuals may have their rights restored after the completion of their sentence.

Candidate Eligibility

Candidates for federal offices must meet minimum age requirements: 25 for the House, 30 for the Senate, and 35 for the presidency. They must be U.S. citizens for specific durations, with presidential candidates requiring natural-born citizenship. Residency requirements also apply, with presidential candidates needing 14 years in the US and congressional candidates residing in their state. Filing procedures include submitting candidacy declarations and financial disclosures to the Federal Election Commission.

These criteria uphold electoral integrity, ensuring compliance with legal standards for participation in U.S. elections.

Constitutional Balance: Republic and Democracy in the United States

The U.S. Constitution establishes the foundation for both the republican and democratic aspects of the American political system. In the republican system, representatives are elected by the people to make decisions on their behalf (Article I). This is evident in the creation of Congress, comprising the Senate and the House of Representatives, with senators initially appointed by state legislatures and now elected by popular vote, and House members directly elected by citizens. Additionally, the Constitution outlines the process for electing the president, originally through the Electoral College system.

In the democratic system, the Constitution guarantees fundamental rights and liberties through the Bill of Rights, including freedom of speech, religion, and assembly, and protections against unreasonable searches and seizures. It also establishes the principle of popular sovereignty, asserting that governmental power resides with the people. Moreover, the Constitution allows for democratic processes such as the amendment process, enabling adaptation to changing societal norms and values through a deliberative process involving the states and the federal government.

Overall, the Constitution combines both republican and democratic elements, ensuring a government that is representative of the people, governed by their consent, and protective of individual rights and freedoms. Historically, the U.S. Constitution has witnessed many amendments related to the electoral law, including:

Section 2, 14th Amendment

Section 2 of the 14th Amendment to the U.S. Constitution addresses apportionment of representatives in Congress. It states that if any state denies the right to vote for any male inhabitants who are a minimum of 21 years of age and are citizens of the United States, except for participation in rebellion or other crime, then the basis of representation in that state will be reduced proportionally. This reduction applies unless the denial of the right to vote is for participation in the rebellion or other crimes. The purpose of this section was to ensure that states did not disenfranchise African American men after the Civil War.

Section 3, 14th Amendment

Section 3 of the 14th Amendment to the U.S. Constitution addresses disqualification from holding office for individuals who have engaged in rebellion or given aid and comfort to the enemies of the United States. It stipulates that any person who has previously taken an oath to support the Constitution of the United States and then engaged in rebellion or aided the enemies of the nation shall be disqualified from holding any office, civil or military, under the United States or any state, unless Congress, by a two-thirds vote of each House, removes such disability.

This section aimed to prevent former Confederate leaders and sympathizers from holding positions of power in the government following the Civil War.

15th Amendment

The 15th Amendment to the U.S. Constitution, ratified in 1870, prohibits the denial of voting rights based on race, color, or previous condition of servitude. It states that "the right of citizens of the United States to vote shall not be denied or abridged by the United States or by any state on account of race, color, or previous condition of servitude." This amendment aimed to grant African American men the right to vote, effectively overturning discriminatory practices such as poll taxes, literacy tests, and intimidation tactics that were used to disenfranchise Black voters in the post-Civil War South. However, despite the 15th Amendment's passage, discriminatory practices persisted for decades, leading to the eventual enactment of additional legislation, such as the Voting Rights Act of 1965, to further protect voting rights for all citizens.

19th Amendment

The 19th Amendment to the U.S. Constitution, ratified in 1920, granted women the right to vote, prohibiting the denial of voting rights based on sex. This landmark amendment marked a significant victory in the fight for gender equality and expanded democracy by ensuring that women had the same voting rights as men. It was the culmination of decades of activism and advocacy by suffragists, who campaigned tirelessly for women's suffrage through protests, lobbying efforts, and civil disobedience. The passage of the 19th Amendment recognized the importance of women's voices and participation in the democratic process, making it a pivotal moment in American history.

22nd Amendment

The 22nd Amendment, ratified in 1951, limits U.S. presidents to two terms in office. It prevents any person from being elected to the presidency more than twice and restricts those who have served more than two years of a term from being elected more than once. This amendment was a response to Franklin D. Roosevelt's four terms, aiming to prevent the accumulation of excessive power and promote regular turnover of leadership. It established the precedent of presidential term limits, ensuring a balance of power within the U.S. government.

26th Amendment

The 26th Amendment, ratified in 1971, lowered the voting age in the United States from 21 to 18. It ensured that citizens aged 18 and older could not be denied the right to vote based on their age. This amendment was a response to the Vietnam War, acknowledging that those old enough to be drafted and serve in the military should also have the right to participate in the democratic process. By enfranchising young adults, the 26th Amendment aimed to promote greater inclusion and representation in the American electoral system.

The Three Powers: Structure of the United States Republican System

The U.S. Republican system is based on a division of powers among three branches of government: the executive, the legislative, and the judicial.

Executive Branch

- **President:** The president is the head of state and government. They are elected every four years through the Electoral College system. Each state is allocated a certain number of electoral votes based on its population, and the candidate who wins the majority of electoral votes nationwide becomes the president. This indirect method of election combines the popular vote within each state to determine the state's electoral votes, and the candidate with the most electoral votes wins the presidency.

- **Vice President:** The vice president is elected on the same ticket as the president and serves as the president of the Senate. In case of the president's incapacity or death, the vice president assumes the role of president.

Legislative Branch

The legislative branch consists of two chambers: the Senate and the House of Representatives.

- **Senate:** Each state has two senators, regardless of its population. Senators are elected to six-year terms, with one-third of the Senate's seats up for election every two years. Senators are elected by the voters of their respective states.

- **House of Representatives:** The number of representatives for each state is based on its population. Members of the House, commonly known as congressmen or congresswomen, are elected to two-year terms. The entire House is up for election every two years, with Representatives chosen by voters in their respective congressional districts.

Judicial Branch

Judges of the federal courts, including the Supreme Court, are appointed by the president and must be confirmed by the Senate. Once appointed, these judges serve for life, unless they choose to retire, resign, or are impeached and removed. This lifelong tenure is intended to shield judges from political pressure, enabling them to make decisions based on the law rather than partisan interests.

The Electoral College Debate

In the U.S. electoral system, Electoral College debate centers on whether the current method of electing the president of the United

States is fair and democratic. Advocates argue that the Electoral College preserves the influence of smaller states, reflecting the federalist structure of the country. They contend that it provides stability and predictability to the election process. However, critics argue that the Electoral College can lead to situations where the winner of the popular vote nationally may not win the presidency, undermining the principle of one person, one vote. They also point out that it encourages candidates to focus on swing states, potentially neglecting the interests of other regions. Additionally, there is concern about the possibility of faithless electors deviating from the popular vote. Critics view the Electoral College as an outdated system that does not align with modern democratic principles. The debate over the Electoral College involves complex considerations of representation, fairness, and the balance of power between states and the federal government. Various proposals for reform or abolition have been suggested, but any changes to the system would require a constitutional amendment, making it a challenging issue to address. Ultimately, the debate over the Electoral College reflects broader questions about the nature of democracy and how best to ensure that the voices of all citizens are heard in the election of their leaders.

Structure and Function

The Electoral College is a system used in the United States to indirectly elect the president and vice president. Each state appoints a number of electors based on its representation in Congress, and these electors vote for the presidential and vice-presidential candidates based on the popular vote in their state. The candidate who receives an absolute majority of 270 electoral votes out of 538 total electoral votes wins the presidency. While it was designed to balance the influence of large and small states, it has faced criticism for potentially allowing the winner of the popular vote to lose the election.

If no candidate reaches the required 270 electoral votes, the 12th Amendment outlines the process for selecting the president. In such a scenario, the House of Representatives convenes to choose the president from the top three candidates, with each state delegation casting one vote. The candidate who receives a majority of state delegation votes (at least 26) is elected president.

Winner-Takes-All System

The winner-takes-all system, utilized in nearly all U.S. states during presidential elections, awards all of a state's electoral votes to the candidate who garners the most popular votes within that state. Only Maine and Nebraska deviate, opting for a proportional allocation based on district-level and statewide results. This method significantly shapes the electoral strategy and outcomes, often amplifying marginal victories where a candidate winning a slight majority in a state, say 51%, captures 100% of the electoral votes, disregarding nearly half the voting population's preference. Consequently, presidential campaigns concentrate their resources and efforts on swing states—those with unpredictable results—while neglecting states with a solid partisan lean. This skewed focus can lead to a national election campaign that overlooks the interests and issues of voters in predictably partisan states.

One of the most contentious aspects of the winner-takes-all system is its potential to create a divergence between the national popular vote and the Electoral College outcome. In instances such as the 2000 and 2016 elections, this led to a president who did not win the most popular votes nationwide, highlighting a critical flaw in the fairness and democratic nature of the electoral process. The discrepancy arises because the Electoral College system weighs states differently, and the all-or-nothing approach can distort the representation of national electoral preferences.

The winner-takes-all rule's impact extends beyond the electoral outcomes to affect voter engagement and public trust in the electoral process. In states where the majority preference is almost certain, voters from the minority or opposing side might feel that their votes are ineffectual, potentially decreasing voter turnout and reducing overall political engagement. The system's tendency to overlook a substantial portion of the electorate raises questions about its adherence to the democratic principle of "one person, one vote."

Despite its role in simplifying electoral allocations and reinforcing federalism by underscoring the importance of states in presidential elections, the winner-takes-all system faces criticism for undermining democratic values. This has spurred debates and movements aimed at reforming or abolishing the Electoral College in favor of a more direct and representative form of presidential election, such as a national popular vote. Such changes are advocated to ensure that the presidency reflects the true will of the people, enhancing democratic legitimacy and voter participation across the country.

This system, widely used in U.S. presidential elections, often leads to significant underrepresentation of minority groups and challenges in ensuring effective governability. It can marginalize racial and ethnic minorities concentrated in areas where their preferences differ from the state majority. This exacerbates feelings of disenfranchisement and decreases political engagement among these groups. Furthermore, the potential for a president to win the Electoral College without securing the popular vote can undermine the legitimacy of their mandate, leading to national divisiveness and governance challenges. Here are some important legislations about the electoral college and indirect election system:

12th Amendment

The 12th Amendment, ratified in 1804, altered the process of electing the president and vice president. It mandated that electors cast separate votes for each office, eliminating the risk of ties. It also established that a candidate must receive an absolute majority of electoral votes to be elected president, and in the event of no majority, contingent elections would be held in the House of Representatives for president and the Senate for vice president. This amendment aimed to address the flaws in the original system, ensuring a smoother and more efficient electoral process in the young American democracy.

23rd Amendment

The 23rd Amendment, ratified in 1961, granted residents of Washington, DC the right to vote in presidential elections by awarding them electoral votes. Prior to this amendment, DC residents were disenfranchised in presidential elections despite paying federal taxes and serving in the military. The amendment gave DC the same number of electoral votes as the least populous state, currently three. It aimed to provide representation to DC residents in the Electoral College, recognizing their status as American citizens and ensuring their participation in the democratic process at the federal level.

24th Amendment

The 24th Amendment, ratified in 1964, abolished the use of poll taxes in federal elections. Poll taxes, which required individuals to pay a fee in order to vote, disproportionately disenfranchised low-income and minority voters. The amendment aimed to eliminate financial barriers to voting and ensure that the right to vote was not contingent upon a person's ability to pay. By prohibiting the use of poll taxes in federal elections, the 24th Amendment furthered the principles of equality and democracy by expanding access to the ballot box for all eligible citizens, regardless of their economic status.

The Primaries and Caucuses Unveiled

The primary elections play a pivotal role as a key platform where political parties can pinpoint and officially select their nominees for the position of presidential candidate. These significant elections occur on a state-by-state basis, including various territories, offering registered voters the chance to participate in the democratic process by casting their votes for their favored candidate within their respective party. The primary season typically spans several months, leading up to the general election, with states holding primaries at different times.

One of the primary purposes of these elections is to help parties identify the most viable candidates to compete in the general election. By allowing party members to participate in selecting their nominee, primaries provide a democratic process for determining who will represent the party on the national stage. Through this process, parties aim to choose candidates who are not only aligned with their core principles but also possess the qualities and appeal necessary to win the presidency.

Some states hold open primaries, where voters can choose which party's primary to participate in regardless of their party affiliation, while others have closed primaries, where only registered members of the party can vote. Additionally, states may allocate delegates proportionally based on the primary results or through a winner-takes-all system.

Caucuses

In addition to primaries, caucuses also play a significant role in the presidential nominating process. Caucuses are meetings held by political parties at the local level, where registered party members gather to discuss and vote for their preferred candidate. These gatherings serve as forums for political participation, allowing individuals to engage directly with the democratic process by voicing their opinions and supporting their chosen candidate.

By participating in the primary and caucus process, individuals have the opportunity to shape the direction of their party and influence the selection of candidates who will champion their interests and values. Moreover, the primary and caucus process allows political parties to refine their campaigns by listening to diverse perspectives and fine-tuning their policy proposals to better serve society as a whole.

Historically, the primary and caucus processes have played a decisive role in shaping presidential elections. For example, in the 2008 Democratic primary, Barack Obama's success in early caucuses in states like Iowa helped propel his campaign forward and ultimately secure the party's nomination.

Similarly, Donald Trump's victories in key primary states during the 2016 Republican primary solidified his position as the party's nominee and eventual president.

Ballot Measures and Referendums

Ballot measures and referendums are direct democratic tools that allow citizens to participate in the political process by directly voting on specific issues or proposals.

Initiatives

Initiatives are a form of ballot measure that allows citizens to propose and vote on new legislation or amendments to state constitutions directly, bypassing the traditional legislative process. This form of direct democracy is a powerful tool that enables the electorate to address and legislate on issues that may be overlooked or avoided by their representatives.

Referendums

Referendums, which are fundamentally akin to ballot measures, are usually centered around the populace casting their votes regarding a particular piece of legislation that has been approved by a governing body, like a state legislature or a city council. Through referendums, citizens are granted the vital chance to either give their consent to or dissent from laws that have been put into effect by their elected officials.

Recalls

Recalls serve as an important democratic process designed to hold elected officials accountable for their actions and decisions. This mechanism allows constituents to intervene if an official's behavior raises concerns or falls short of public expectations.

Ballot measures, referendums, and recalls are tools of direct democracy allowing citizens to influence legislation and official positions through petitions and voting. Initiatives and referendums require gathering signatures to qualify for ballots, where they are directly voted on by the public. Initiatives can originate from citizens, while referendums might also be initiated by legislative bodies. Recalls, aimed at removing elected officials before their term ends, also necessitate collecting sufficient petition signatures to trigger a special election. Through these processes, citizens actively engage by signing petitions, campaigning, and voting, thereby directly shaping policies and governance.

Real-Life Examples

Initiatives

- **Topic:** Legalization of Marijuana, California, 2016.

- **Proponents:** Advocacy groups like California NORML and the Marijuana Policy Project.

- **Outcome:** Approved with 57% of the vote.

- **Impact:** Legalized recreational marijuana for adults over 21, impacting the criminal justice system and generating tax revenue.

- **Legal Framework:** Governed by Article II, Section 8 of the California Constitution.

Referendums

- **Topic:** Brexit Referendum, United Kingdom, 2016.

- **Caller:** UK government under Prime Minister David Cameron.

- **Outcome:** 52% voted for the UK to leave the European Union.

- **Impact:** Led to economic instability, altered trade relations, and ongoing debates about national identity.

- **Legal Framework:** Enabled by the European Union Referendum Act 2015.

Recalls

- **Topic:** Recall of Governor Gray Davis, California, 2003.

- **Proponents:** Citizen activists led by Ted Costa.

- **Outcome:** 55.4% supported the recall, leading to Davis's removal.

- **Impact:** Resulted in Arnold Schwarzenegger becoming governor, changing state policies and drawing global attention to California politics.

- **Legal Framework:** Outlined in Sections 11000–11110 of the California Elections Code.

Political Polling

Polls are surveys that measure public opinion on political candidates, issues, and policies. They help candidates understand voter sentiment and shape their campaigns. However, polls can influence voter behavior, creating a "bandwagon effect" where people support the perceived frontrunner. Polling companies may have biases due to affiliations or financial interests, potentially distorting results. They're used in campaigns and lobbying to sway public opinion, which can both inform and manipulate voters.

In recent presidential elections, polls haven't always accurately predicted outcomes, as seen in 2016, when many underestimated Donald Trump's support. Despite their flaws, polls provide valuable insights into voter preferences. However, they should be evaluated alongside other factors and not solely relied upon for voting decisions.

The Future of Election Technology

Electronic voting, or e-voting, refers to the range of technologies employed for casting and counting votes, including direct-recording electronic (DRE) voting machines, online voting systems, and optical scanning devices. These innovative methods signify a departure from the conventional paper-based voting setups, in which ballots are typically filled out manually and then counted by hand.

Comparison of Electronic and Traditional Voting

Electronic voting enhances accessibility, allowing voters with disabilities better access to voting technology and enabling quicker tabulation of results compared to traditional voting. Traditional methods require physical polling places and manual ballot marking, which may be less accessible for some voters and typically result in slower vote counting. In terms of accuracy and transparency, electronic voting reduces human error in the counting of votes; however, the lack of a paper trail can complicate efforts to audit and verify results. In contrast, traditional voting, while prone to human error during counting, generally allows for easier verification through the availability of physical ballots, thus enhancing transparency.

Advantages and Disadvantages

Electronic voting offers several advantages, including efficiency with faster processing and real-time results, potential cost reductions over time in ballot printing and transportation, and improved accessibility for people with disabilities and those living abroad. However, it also comes with significant disadvantages. These systems are vulnerable to hacking and cyber-attacks, the initial setup costs for electronic systems are high, and there are widespread concerns over their reliability and susceptibility to tampering, which can diminish public trust in the electoral process.

Risk of Fraud and Historical Examples

In the United States, allegations of electronic voting fraud have emerged in several elections, notably during the 2004 presidential election where concerns about the integrity of electronic voting machines in Ohio were raised, though no substantial evidence supported claims of deliberate manipulation.

In Russia's 2011 parliamentary elections, reports of electoral fraud were widespread, including allegations of vote rigging and ballot stuffing. While electronic voting systems were not the primary method, they were utilized in some regions. Accusations against the government of manipulating electronic voting results led to protests and international condemnation.

Estonia, known for its advanced electronic voting system, faced scrutiny in the 2007 parliamentary elections. Concerns arose about the system's security, as vulnerabilities were identified that could allow hackers to tamper with votes or compromise results. While no widespread fraud was uncovered, the incident emphasized the need for robust security measures.

In Brazil's 2018 presidential election, allegations of fraud emerged, particularly regarding electronic voting machines. Critics raised concerns about reliability and potential manipulation of results. Though no conclusive evidence of widespread fraud was found, the accusations fueled public distrust in the electoral process.

Costs and Logistics

When considering the implementation of electronic voting systems, it is important to acknowledge the substantial initial investment required for purchasing the necessary hardware, software, and providing comprehensive training. While these upfront costs may appear daunting, supporters of electronic voting systems highlight the potential long-term benefits, suggesting that they could lead to reduced expenditures related to the production, distribution, and tabulation of paper ballots. On the other hand, opponents argue that the continuous maintenance and updates essential for electronic systems entail ongoing expenses that might surpass any savings realized in the future. Ultimately, the decision to adopt electronic voting systems hinges on weighing these initial and recurring costs against the advantages they offer in terms of efficiency and accuracy.

Chapter 4:

Down-Ballot Voting

Down-ballot voting, which is crucial for shaping local communities and governance structures, involves the practice of voting for candidates or initiatives in an election that follow higher-profile races such as presidential, gubernatorial, or senatorial contests. These down-ticket ballots encompass a wide range of positions, including those at the local and state levels, such as mayoralties, city councils, school boards, judgeships, and various ballot measures like initiatives and referendums.

By participating in down-ballot voting, citizens have the opportunity to directly impact and influence policies and decision-making processes at the grassroots level, making their voices heard on issues that affect their day-to-day lives and communities.

Understanding the impact of down-ballot voting is crucial for democracy. These elections determine local and state-level representatives who shape policies affecting communities directly. By participating, citizens ensure their voices are heard at all levels of government, fostering accountability and transparency. Many policies impacting daily life, like education and healthcare, are decided at these levels. Down-ballot voting maintains checks and balances between federal, state, and local power, preventing any one level from dominating. It promotes diversity and inclusion in governance by electing representatives reflecting community demographics.

Additionally, it encourages civic engagement, as informed citizens are more likely to participate in elections. Overall, comprehending the significance of down-ballot voting leads to a more vibrant and representative democracy, where citizens actively shape their communities and hold elected officials accountable for their actions.

The Diversity of Down-Ballot Races

Down-ballot races encompass various positions and issues at the local, state, and judicial levels. Within these races, individuals compete for roles such as city council members, state legislators, and judges.

Local Races

In local races, candidates vie for positions such as mayor, city council member, county commissioner, school board member, and sheriff. Each role carries distinct responsibilities, from leading the local government and crafting laws, to managing county services, overseeing public schools, and ensuring public safety.

State Races

In state races, candidates compete for roles like governor, state legislator, attorney general, secretary of state, and treasurer.

These officials play vital roles in implementing and shaping state laws and policies, representing the state in legal matters, overseeing elections and state records, and managing state finances and investments.

Judicial Races

In judicial races, candidates compete for various positions, such as judgeships and district attorney. Judgeships encompass roles in both trial and appellate courts, while district attorneys prosecute criminal cases on behalf of the state.

Factors Shaping Voter Choices

Down-ballot voting is influenced by several key factors: party affiliation and straight-ticket voting, candidate characteristics and campaign strategies, and voter demographics and turnout.

Party affiliation plays a significant role in down-ballot voting behavior. Many voters align themselves with a particular party and vote for all candidates from that party, known as straight-ticket voting. This simplifies the voting process for those who may not be familiar with down-ballot candidates, relying on party loyalty rather than individual candidate qualifications.

Party affiliation is not the sole determinant of down-ballot voting. Some voters split their tickets by selecting candidates from different parties based on individual qualities or local issues. Independent voters, not aligned with any party, also impact down-ballot races by considering candidates' platforms and qualifications.

Candidate characteristics and campaign strategies are crucial influences. Candidates with strong leadership qualities, relevant experience, and clear visions for their offices are more likely to attract voters. Effective campaign strategies, such as grassroots efforts and targeted advertising, can sway undecided voters and mobilize support.

Visibility and name recognition are vital in down-ballot races where candidates have limited resources. Engagement with voters through events, debates, and social media can boost visibility. Positive media coverage and endorsements further enhance a candidate's credibility.

Voter demographics and turnout rates significantly impact down-ballot elections. Certain groups, such as older adults and affluent individuals, are more likely to vote in local races. This disparity can influence outcomes, especially in close contests or low-turnout areas.

Demographic shifts within communities create opportunities for candidates to appeal to emerging voter blocs. Prioritizing issues relevant to diverse groups, like education and healthcare, can resonate with voters and build support coalitions.

In summary, down-ballot voting is influenced by a complex interplay of factors. While party affiliation and candidate visibility are significant, individual candidate qualities, issue priorities, and demographic shifts also shape voter decisions. Understanding these dynamics is crucial for candidates, campaigns, and voters to effectively participate in down-ballot races and the democratic process.

The Impact of Down-Ballot Voting on Democracy

Down-ballot voting, often overlooked in favor of higher-profile races, significantly shapes democracy by influencing representation, policy, and checks and balances in government.

Firstly, down-ballot voting ensures diverse representation in elected offices. While presidential and gubernatorial races garner attention, local and state-level positions like mayor and city council are equally crucial. These roles directly impact communities, making down-ballot voting vital for ensuring diverse voices are heard in decision-making processes. By participating, voters elect representatives reflecting their community's demographics, values, and interests, fostering inclusivity and diversity in government bodies.

Secondly, down-ballot voting holds significant policy implications at the local and state levels. Many policies directly affecting citizens' daily lives, such as education and public safety, are crafted and implemented at these levels. Thus, participating allows citizens to shape policies addressing their communities' unique needs and challenges. Elected officials influence laws, resource allocation, and program implementation, enabling voters to steer policy directions towards issues like affordable housing and environmental protection.

Lastly, down-ballot voting maintains checks and balances in government. While federal elections dominate discourse, local and state governments counterbalance federal power. Through down-ballot voting, citizens elect officials serving as checks on executive authority and ensuring governance accountability. These officials oversee law enforcement, public administration, and budgeting, preventing potential power abuses and ensuring government responsiveness. Additionally, down-ballot voting prevents any single branch or level of government from overpowering others, preserving essential checks and balances fundamental to democracy.

Many winners of down-ballot races often use their experience and success as a springboard to higher offices. This phenomenon is often referred to as the "political ladder" or "political pipeline." For example, individuals elected to positions like city council members, state legislators, or even mayors may later run for higher offices such as governor, senator, or even president. Likewise, successful candidates for state judgeships or attorney general positions may be considered for federal judicial appointments or run for positions like state governor or U.S. senator in the future. Therefore, down-ballot races serve not only as an opportunity to influence local governance but also as a pathway for aspiring politicians to advance to higher levels of leadership and potentially shape broader policies on state and national levels.

Empowering Voters in Down-Ballot Races

Strategies for informed voting are pivotal in ensuring effective democratic participation, particularly in down-ballot races where candidates and issues may receive less attention. These strategies include researching down-ballot candidates, evaluating their platforms and qualifications, and recognizing the importance of local media and community engagement.

Researching down-ballot candidates is essential. While high-profile races may garner extensive media coverage, down-ballot contests often receive less attention, necessitating proactive efforts by voters to gather information. Research methods can include visiting candidates' websites, attending candidate forums or debates, and reading news articles and endorsements. By delving into candidates' backgrounds, experiences, and positions on key issues, voters can make more informed decisions at the ballot box.

Evaluating candidate platforms and qualifications is crucial. Understanding where candidates stand on important issues and how their policy proposals align with voters' values and priorities is vital for informed decision-making. Voters should consider candidates' positions on a range of topics, including education, healthcare, economic development, and public safety. Additionally, assessing candidates' qualifications, such as their professional experience, leadership abilities, and community involvement, provides insight into their suitability for office.

Recognizing the importance of local media and community engagement enhances informed voting. Local newspapers, radio stations, and community organizations play vital roles in disseminating information about down-ballot races and candidates. Engaging with these local sources of information, attending candidate events, and participating in community forums and discussions can help voters gain deeper insights into candidates and issues affecting their communities. Seeking recommendations and insights from neighbors, friends, and community leaders further enriches voters' understanding and perspective.

Case Studies and Success Stories

Down-ballot races wield significant influence over governance, often shaping policies that directly impact communities. Highlighting their importance are notable instances where seemingly small races sparked significant change.

One such example is the 2018 Democratic primary for New York's 14th Congressional District. Alexandria Ocasio-Cortez's grassroots campaign, advocating progressive ideals, toppled incumbent Joseph

Crowley. This victory underscored the potency of grassroots organizing in down-ballot contests, signaling a shift in the political landscape.

Similarly, Kim Foxx's bid for Cook County State's Attorney in 2016 demonstrated the power of grassroots movements. Supported by community activists, Foxx secured the Democratic nomination and later the general election, marking a watershed moment for criminal justice reform.

Grassroots initiatives have also influenced broader policy discussions. For instance, campaigns for same-sex marriage legalization across various states showcased the impact of community engagement and coalition building. These efforts, fueled by door-to-door canvassing and education drives, led to historic victories, advancing equality nationwide.

Environmental advocacy further exemplifies grassroots success. From fracking bans to renewable energy mandates, local ballot initiatives have spurred tangible environmental policy changes. By harnessing technology and social media, activists have amplified their reach, engaging diverse audiences and mobilizing support.

In summary, down-ballot races serve as vital arenas for grassroots activism, shaping governance and policy at the local and national levels. Through strategic organizing, coalition building, and persistence, grassroots movements have the potential to influence outcomes and drive meaningful progress in their communities.

Chapter 5:

The Evolution of Political Campaigns

From the early days of door-to-door canvassing to the modern era of social media saturation, this chapter traces the metamorphosis of political strategies in the USA. Each era, marked by its unique tools and tactics, reflects not only the changing landscape of technology but also the evolving nature of democracy itself.

Political Milestones Throughout American History

The political evolution of the United States is a complex tapestry woven over centuries, marked by pivotal milestones, conflicts, resolutions, and the continuous struggle for civil and political rights. From its inception as a fledgling nation seeking independence to its transformation into a global superpower, the United States has navigated through numerous challenges and triumphs, shaping its political landscape along the way.

1776: Declaration of Independence—The foundational moment in American history, where thirteen British colonies declared their independence from British rule, paving the way for the birth of the United States of America.

1787: Constitutional Convention—Delegates from the thirteen states convened in Philadelphia to draft the United States Constitution, establishing the framework for the federal government, including the separation of powers and the system of checks and balances.

1789: Ratification of the Bill of Rights—The first ten amendments to the Constitution were ratified, guaranteeing essential civil liberties such as freedom of speech, religion, and the right to a fair trial.

1803: Louisiana Purchase—President Thomas Jefferson's acquisition of the Louisiana Territory from France doubled the size of the United States, setting the stage for westward expansion.

1861–1865: Civil War—A defining moment in American history, the Civil War erupted over issues of states' rights and slavery, resulting in the abolition of slavery with the passage of the 13th Amendment and the preservation of the Union.

1865–1877: Reconstruction Era—Following the Civil War, the United States underwent a period of rebuilding and social upheaval, marked by efforts to integrate formerly enslaved African Americans into society and the political landscape.

1890s: Progressive Era—A period of social and political reform aimed at addressing the excesses of the Gilded Age, including the regulation of big business, labor rights, and women's suffrage.

1919–1933: Prohibition Era—The 18th Amendment to the Constitution prohibited the manufacture, sale, and transportation of alcoholic beverages, leading to a rise in organized crime and ultimately culminating in its repeal with the 21st Amendment.

1929–1939: Great Depression—The worst economic downturn in U.S. history, characterized by widespread unemployment, bank failures, and poverty, leading to the implementation of New Deal programs by President Franklin D. Roosevelt to provide relief, recovery, and reform.

1950s–1960s: Civil Rights Movement—A transformative period marked by grassroots activism and legal challenges aimed at ending racial segregation and discrimination, culminating in landmark legislation such as the Civil Rights Act of 1964 and the Voting Rights Act of 1965.

1960s–1970s: Vietnam War and Counterculture Movement—A divisive conflict that sparked widespread protests and demonstrations against U.S. involvement in Southeast Asia, reflecting a broader cultural shift towards social liberalism and youth activism.

1970s–1980s: Conservative Resurgence—The rise of conservative politics, exemplified by the election of Ronald Reagan in 1980, marked a shift towards deregulation, tax cuts, and a more assertive foreign policy stance.

1990s: End of the Cold War—The collapse of the Soviet Union and the end of the Cold War reshaped the geopolitical landscape, solidifying the United States' position as the world's sole superpower.

2000s: War on Terror—The September 11, 2001, terrorist attacks prompted a global campaign against terrorism, leading to military interventions in Afghanistan and Iraq, as well as controversial domestic surveillance programs.

2010s: Polarization and Gridlock—Increasing political polarization and partisan gridlock characterized much of the 2010s, as ideological divisions deepened and compromise became increasingly elusive.

2020s: Pandemic and Renewed Calls for Social Justice—The COVID-19 pandemic exposed deep-seated inequalities in American society, while renewed calls for racial justice following the killing of George Floyd sparked nationwide protests and calls for systemic reform.

The United States has faced many challenges, from its core values of freedom and fairness to ongoing issues of unfairness and injustice. But it's this ongoing fight for improvement that shapes the country's political journey.

The Evolution of American Political Parties

The Dual Nature of American Politics

The two-party system in the United States means that there are two main political groups: the Democrats and the Republicans. This setup has some advantages and disadvantages.

One good thing about it is that it brings stability and clarity. People know what each party stands for, which can make voting easier. This system also helps keep things balanced in government, as control tends to switch between the two parties. This balance can encourage compromise and smooth governance. Moreover, it gives people a sense of belonging. They feel connected to their chosen party and are more likely to get involved in politics, which is good for democracy.

However, there are downsides too. One big problem is that it limits diversity. Smaller parties and independent candidates struggle to get attention, so voters don't always have many options. This lack of choice can make the political landscape feel narrow and stifled. Also, the two-party system can lead to polarization and gridlock. When the two parties have very different ideas, it's hard for them to agree on anything. This can make it tough to solve important issues and get things done in government.

The Dynamics of Alternating Power

The alternating-party system in the USA embodies the cyclical exchange of political power between the two major parties, the Democrats and the Republicans. This system ensures regular turnover of leadership, with each party taking its turn in governing through electoral victories.

Over two centuries of uninterrupted democracy, this system has provided a stable framework for governance. It facilitates a peaceful transition of power, preventing the entrenchment of any single party and thereby safeguarding against authoritarian tendencies. By allowing both parties to have opportunities to govern, the alternating-party system fosters a sense of inclusivity and representation, ensuring that diverse interests and viewpoints are considered in decision-making processes.

This system promotes accountability and transparency in government. With each party knowing it will face the electorate again, there is a built-in incentive to deliver on campaign promises and govern responsibly. Opposition parties serve as watchdogs, scrutinizing the actions of the ruling party and providing checks and balances to prevent abuses of power.

However, the alternating-party system also presents challenges. It can lead to policy inconsistencies and gridlock when parties have divergent agendas and struggle to find common ground. Additionally, some critics argue that the dominance of the two major parties stifles political diversity and limits the representation of alternative voices.

While the alternating-party system has its drawbacks, it has generally served the United States well by upholding democratic principles, promoting accountability, and ensuring a peaceful transfer of power.

Timeline of Political Party Evolution in the United States

Time Period	Political Parties	Main Referents
1776–1789	None	Founding Fathers: George Washington, Thomas Jefferson, John Adams, Benjamin Franklin, Alexander Hamilton, and James Madison.

1789–1824	Federalist Party vs. Democratic-Republican Party	• Federalist: Alexander Hamilton, John Marshall, and John Adams. • Democratic-Republican: Thomas Jefferson, James Monroe, and Aaron Burr.
1824–1836	Democratic-Republican Party vs. National Republican Party	• Democratic-Republican: Thomas Jefferson, Andrew Jackson, and John Quincy Adams. • National Republican: Henry Clay, John Marshall, and Daniel Webster.
1836–1854	Democratic Party vs. Whig Party	• Democratic Party: Andrew Jackson, Martin Van Buren, Stephen A. Douglas, and Franklin Pierce. • Whig Party: Daniel Webster, William Henry Harrison, and Zachary Taylor.
1854–1856	Emergence of the Republican Party	• Abraham Lincoln, Horace Greeley, Charles Sumner, and John C. Frémont.

1856– Present	Democratic Party vs. Republican Party		• Democratic Party: Andrew Johnson, Grover Cleveland, Woodrow Wilson, Franklin D. Roosevelt, John F. Kennedy, Bill Clinton, Barack Obama, and Joe Biden. • Republican Party: Abraham Lincoln, Theodore Roosevelt, Dwight D. Eisenhower, Ronald Reagan, George H. W. Bush, George W. Bush, and Donald Trump.

Presidents of the United States: Terms, Parties, and Congressional Landscape

President	Period	Party	Congress Composition
George Washington	1789–1797	Independent	Federalist (Senate) / Federalist-Republican (House)
John Adams	1797–1801	Federalist	Federalist (Senate & House)
Thomas Jefferson	1801–1809	Democratic-Republican	Democratic-Republican (Senate & House)

James Madison	1809–1817	Democratic-Republican	Democratic-Republican (Senate & House)
James Monroe	1817–1825	Democratic-Republican	Democratic-Republican (Senate & House)
John Quincy Adams	1825–1829	Democratic-Republican/National Republican	Democratic-Republican/National Republican (Senate & House)
Andrew Jackson	1829–1837	Democratic	Democratic (Senate & House)
Martin Van Buren	1837–1841	Democratic	Democratic (Senate) / Whig (House)
William Henry Harrison	1841	Whig	Whig (Senate & House)
John Tyler	1841–1845	Whig	Whig (Senate & House)
James K. Polk	1845–1849	Democratic	Democratic (Senate & House)
Zachary Taylor	1849–1850	Whig	Whig (Senate & House)
Millard Fillmore	1850–1853	Whig	Whig (Senate & House)

Franklin Pierce	1853–1857	Democratic	Democratic (Senate & House)
James Buchanan	1857–1861	Democratic	Democratic (Senate & House)
Abraham Lincoln	1861–1865	Republican	Republican (Senate & House)
Andrew Johnson	1865–1869	National Union (Democrat)	Republican (Senate & House) / National Union (Senate) / Democratic (House)
Ulysses S. Grant	1869–1877	Republican	Republican (Senate & House)
Rutherford B. Hayes	1877–1881	Republican	Republican (Senate & House)
James A. Garfield	1881	Republican	Republican (Senate & House)
Chester A. Arthur	1881–1885	Republican	Republican (Senate & House)
Grover Cleveland	1885–1889	Democratic	Democratic (Senate & House)
Benjamin Harrison	1889–1893	Republican	Republican (Senate & House)
Grover Cleveland	1893–1897	Republican	Democratic (Senate & House)

William McKinley	1897–1901	Republican	Republican (Senate & House)
Theodore Roosevelt	1901–1909	Republican	Republican (Senate & House)
William Howard Taft	1909–1913	Republican	Republican (Senate & House)
Woodrow Wilson	1913–1921	Democratic	Democratic (Senate & House)
Warren G. Harding	1921–1923	Republican	Republican (Senate & House)
Calvin Coolidge	1923–1929	Republican	Republican (Senate & House)
Herbert Hoover	1929–1933	Republican	Republican (Senate & House)
Franklin D. Roosevelt	1933–1945	Democratic	Democratic (Senate & House)
Harry S. Truman	1945–1953	Democratic	Democratic (Senate & House)
Dwight D. Eisenhower	1953–1961	Republican	Republican (Senate & House)
John F. Kennedy	1961–1963	Democratic	Democratic (Senate & House)

President	Years	Party	Congress
Lyndon B. Johnson	1963–1969	Democratic	Democratic (Senate & House)
Richard Nixon	1969–1974	Republican	Democratic (Senate) / Republican (House)
Gerald Ford	1974–1977	Republican	Democratic (Senate) / Republican (House)
Jimmy Carter	1977–1981	Democratic	Democratic (Senate & House)
Ronald Reagan	1981–1989	Republican	Republican (Senate) / Democratic (House)
George H. W. Bush	1989–1993	Republican	Democratic (Senate & House)
Bill Clinton	1993–2001	Democratic	Democratic (Senate & House)
George W. Bush	2001–2009	Republican	Democratic (Senate) / Republican (House)
Barack Obama	2009–2017	Democratic	Democratic (Senate) / Republican (House)
Donald Trump	2017–2021	Republican	Republican (Senate & House)
Joe Biden	2021–	Democratic	Democratic (Senate) / Republican (House)

America's Dual-Party Landscape: Origins and Implication

There is almost no mention of other parties from the American political scene except for the "Republicans" and the "Democrats," which raises questions about the reason for this and the nature of party life in the country.

Since the middle of the nineteenth century, when the Republican Party was founded, competition has been concentrated between the latter and the Democratic Party, which was founded in its current form in 1828, until the political system in the country became described as "two-party rule."

"Two-party rule" in the United States is not established in the Constitution. Still, it is a natural product of the electoral system, which is based on the rule of "the winner takes all the seats" of the electoral district, as is the case in the parliamentary ballot, or the state's balance in the Electoral College, as in the competition for presidency.

This would focus the competition between only two strong parties, as the opposition movements would unite behind the most powerful of them, to overthrow the ruling party, while the movements closest to the latter would rally behind it to preserve its rule, which would destroy the chances of other parties and candidates.

This reflects a sharp polarization in American society, especially in its early days, between a South demanding a confederal system in which states enjoy greater powers, versus a North seeking to strengthen federal centralization. This was followed, after the Civil War (1861–1865), by polarization between conservatism and liberalism to this day.

Third Parties in the United States: A History of Struggle and Influence

Third parties in the United States have a long and varied history that dates back to the country's founding, with a consistent struggle to gain significant traction in national elections due to the entrenched dominance of the two major parties, the Democrats and the Republicans. This challenge has persisted despite occasional bursts of momentum driven by unique candidates or shifting political climates over the years.

Throughout United States history, third parties have emerged at pivotal junctures in response to a diverse array of compelling social, economic, and political issues. These parties, such as the Populist Party during the late 19th century, the Progressive Party in the early 20th century, and more contemporarily, the Libertarian Party, the Green Party, and the Constitution Party, have provided alternative platforms and perspectives that have challenged the dominance of the two major political parties.

Despite their oftentimes fervent supporters and sporadic victories in smaller-scale elections, third parties have encountered a multitude of challenges when it comes to making an impact in national political contests. The overarching winner-takes-all electoral system, characterized by awarding electoral votes or seats based on a mere plurality rather than proportional representation, presents a formidable barrier for third-party candidates seeking to secure a meaningful presence. Moreover, the entrenched dominance of the two major political entities provides them with considerable advantages in crucial realms such as fundraising, media exposure, and institutional backing, further compounding the obstacles faced by alternative political groups trying to break into the mainstream political scene.

In recent electoral events, third parties have consistently faced challenges in gaining substantial traction among voters. For instance, during the 2020 presidential election, minor political entities, such as Jo Jorgensen from the Libertarian Party and Howie Hawkins representing the Green Party, struggled to attract significant support, garnering only a small fraction of the overall popular vote. The lion's share of the electorate overwhelmingly favored candidates from the two dominant parties, namely the Democrats and the Republicans.

When considering the distribution of seats in Congress, it is evident that third parties have encountered challenges in gaining substantial representation. Over the course of history, intermittent instances of third-party presence in Congress have been recorded, yet such occurrences have remained infrequent and transitory. Presently, the U.S. Senate lacks any members affiliated with third parties, with only a handful of independents aligning themselves with one of the major political parties. Within the House of Representatives, sporadic appearances by third-party representatives have been observed, albeit with consistent struggles to exert robust influence given their limited numbers.

Despite their relatively smaller presence in the political landscape, third parties possess the potential to significantly impact the broader dialogue and the policies pursued by the major political players. When third parties advocate for important causes like environmental protection, safeguarding civil liberties, or advocating for electoral reforms, their influence often prompts the major parties to incorporate these ideals into their own agendas as a response to the demands of the general public. This dynamic exchange between third parties and the major political entities paves the way for a more comprehensive and inclusive representation of societal concerns within the political sphere.

Political Party Platforms

Exploring America's Political Spectrum

In the United States, the Democratic and Republican Parties dominate the political landscape, each with distinct platforms and policy priorities. The Democratic Party, considered center-left, advocates for progressive policies on social issues, healthcare, environmental protection, civil rights, and income equality. Meanwhile, the Republican Party, positioned center-right, supports conservative principles such as limited government intervention in the economy, lower taxes, free markets, and a strong national defense. Independents, who do not align with either major party, may hold seats in Congress and caucus with one of the major parties, embodying diverse ideologies and policy positions.

Other political parties, although less influential, contribute to the American political spectrum. The Libertarian Party champions minimal government intervention in both economic and social affairs, prioritizing individual freedom, free markets, civil liberties, and non-interventionist foreign policy. The Green Party focuses on environmental sustainability, social justice, and grassroots democracy, advocating for policies like renewable energy and universal healthcare. Emphasizing adherence to the Constitution and traditional values, the Constitution Party often aligns with conservative Christian principles.

Despite their varied perspectives, these smaller parties struggle to gain significant traction in national elections due to the dominance of the two-party system and institutional barriers. While they occasionally elect members to local or state offices, their representation in Congress is limited. Nevertheless, these parties offer alternative viewpoints and represent a diverse range of ideologies within American politics, contributing to the richness and diversity of the political discourse.

Timeline of U.S. Political Party Platform Evolution

Period	Major Shifts in Party Platforms
Early 1800s	The **Democratic-Republicans**, a political faction championed by Thomas Jefferson, stood firmly in favor of states' rights, promoting agrarianism as their ideal economic model, and advocating for a strict interpretation of the Constitution to limit the federal government's powers. Contrasting this stance, the **Federalists**, spearheaded by Alexander Hamilton, vigorously supported the concept of a robust central government, actively promoting industrial development and subscribing to a loose interpretation of the Constitution to grant more flexibility in governance.

Mid–1800s	The **Democrats** of the era began to gravitate towards the principles of Jacksonian democracy, championing the everyday citizen, supporting the expansion of the nation to the west, and advocating for a governmental approach with minimal federal interference. Conversely, the **Whigs** emerged in direct response to Jackson, prioritizing economic advancement, pushing for internal infrastructure enhancements, and the creation of a centralized banking system.
Late 1800s	During the late-19th century, the emergence of the **Republican Party** marked a significant political shift, as they positioned themselves as a staunch advocate for the abolition of slavery, championing civil rights and pushing for economic modernization. In contrast, the **Democratic Party** at the time was largely influenced by Southern interests, maintaining a stance that prioritized states' rights and the preservation of the institution of slavery.
Early 1900s	During the Progressive Movement, both the **Republican** and **Democratic** parties embraced progressive reforms aimed at addressing key societal issues. **Republicans** leaned towards supporting business interests, emphasizing policies that favored economic growth, whereas **Democrats** focused on championing progressive social and economic agendas. Labor rights enforcement and the implementation of social welfare initiatives were central components of their reform efforts.

1920s–1930s	During Franklin D. Roosevelt's presidency, **Democrats** adopted New Deal policies that revolutionized the American socio-economic landscape. This included the implementation of Social Security, active government involvement in the economy, and the championing of labor rights. In contrast, **Republicans** initially resisted many New Deal programs, only to gradually integrate certain elements into their policies during Eisenhower's administration.
1950s–1960s	During the civil rights movement, **Democrats** solidified their commitment by advocating for desegregation and voting rights, ultimately aligning themselves with the cause. On the other hand, **Republicans** shifted their appeal by opposing civil rights legislation and emphasizing states' rights, attracting a conservative Southern white demographic in the process.
1980s–1990s	**Republicans** solidified their identity as the proponents of Reagan conservatism, championing the principles of limited government intervention, reduced taxation, deregulation of industries, and a firm stance on national security. Meanwhile, **Democrats** underwent a transformation during Bill Clinton's era, gravitating towards more moderate stances characterized by an emphasis on free trade policies and the implementation of welfare reform measures.
2000s–Present	**Republicans** have maintained their focus on conservative policies such as implementing tax cuts, supporting deregulation, and advocating for a strong foreign policy stance. On the other hand, **Democrats** have shifted towards more progressive positions, particularly in the areas of social issues, healthcare reform, environmental conservation, and addressing income inequality.

Campaign Finance

A political campaign, a planned and calculated endeavor orchestrated by a candidate or political party, serves as a pivotal strategic tool aimed at persuading the electorate to extend their support towards the particular candidate or endorse their policies and ideologies. This multifaceted approach typically comprises an array of dynamic activities, such as engaging public speeches, energizing rallies, advertisements, spirited debates, and canvassing efforts. Through a deliberate orchestration of these events, campaigns are designed to amplify visibility, mobilize ardent supporters, and ultimately sway the opinions of indecisive voters. Consequently, they hold immense significance in shaping the political landscape of a nation, functioning as an indispensable channel for disseminating crucial information about candidates and key issues, fostering active democratic participation amongst citizens, and wielding a profound influence on public sentiment and decision-making.

The Cost of Electoral Campaigns

In 2020, Americans spent nearly $15 billion on election campaigns, $6 billion of which went to the presidential elections, while $9 billion went to the congressional, gubernatorial, and other local elections (Open Secrets, 2021). Recent estimates anticipate that the scale of spending during the upcoming 2024 elections will surpass a staggering $20 billion, signifying a significant increase in financial resources allocated towards this pivotal political event.

Despite the democracy, transparency, and freedom that the American system enjoys, this system has not yet found a legitimate solution that can eliminate the influence of the role of money in elections. What they have been able to come up with is a set of serious laws that regulate these relationships between donors and candidates, and set rules and limits for spending; but the influence of money continues to be a recurring nightmare with every election cycle, whether presidential or congressional.

As for transparency regarding who is funding candidates, there are many websites with great credibility, including the Open Secrets website, where you can search by name, profession, or the amount donated, and where these people live. There is a Federal Election Commission website that provides a lot of data and information about who is funding whom.

Who Regulates the Financing of U.S. Elections?

The establishment of the Federal Election Commission in 1974 as a neutral body that legislates electoral processes and supervises the commitment of candidates and parties to the required transparency and publicity came as an important step in this difficult path.

One of the most important achievements of this committee is that it obliges all candidates to announce the identity of donors and the amount of each one's contribution. It also publishes consolidated reports on the amounts provided to each candidate and makes them available to the people for review.

The committee consists of six commissioners, three from each of the two main parties, the Democratic and the Republican, which sometimes makes it difficult to reach effective decisions for the committee.

American Election Financing Process

There are three basic and unconventional rules for elections, through which the complexities of financing American elections can be deciphered:

- **First:** There are no limits on political spending, by the First Amendment to the U.S. Constitution as interpreted by the Supreme Court. No group or individual can be told how much he or she can spend on political affairs, including financing elections or supporting candidates. There are no laws that limit political spending, but there are laws and rules for limiting an individual or group's contribution to granting a candidate or party a certain amount of money, to prevent and limit the dimensions of quasi-corruption.

- **Second:** Almost all funding at the federal level comes from private sources, and there is some limited public funding for candidates. However, because of these numbers' limitations, the candidates do not care to use the public funds allocated to them, especially with the high cost of running elections in recent decades.

- **Third:** Spending by independent groups, which do not associate themselves with a candidate or political party, is increasing quickly.

Sources of Funding for US Elections

There are three primary sources, and one non-primary source. The primary sources are:

- Political parties provide money to candidates, can finance advertising in the media, and can help mobilize voters.

- Political action committees (PACs) are gatherings sponsored by corporations, unions, or activist groups, where they raise money and give it to candidates' campaigns.

- Individual donors can give unlimited amounts to as many candidates and parties as they want.

There are independent groups called (Super PACs) that do not directly contribute to financing the elections. Instead, they spend whatever money they want directly to help the candidate by running ads, putting up banners, and distributing promotional materials, but they cannot communicate directly with the candidate, as that is considered a contribution, and this has limits.

Limits on Financial Contributions Supporting a Candidate or Party

There are some restrictions on contributions to candidates and parties. Under federal law, a person can donate up to a maximum of $3,300 per election. A person can give to the same candidate in a primary and general election, for a total of $6,600. A person can also give a party up to $41,000 per election cycle (Federal Election Commission, 2023).

As for political action committees (PACs), each committee can donate $5,000. For example, if you are the head of a company or a union leader, you can collect this amount of money and give it to your favorite candidate or party (Federal Election Commission, 2023).

Election financing rules also allow people to collect donations from friends and acquaintances within the indicated limits, and present them to the candidate or party. This is a common practice called (bundling), where an important person organizes a party at his home and collects a lot of money from his wealthy friends, then delivers this money to the candidate or the party.

Laws prohibit receiving any donations from any non-American persons or entities, while permanent residency holders (as taxpayers) can legally participate in financing elections, despite their inability to vote in elections until after they obtain American citizenship.

It is worth noting that everyone can contribute to election campaigns: individuals, persons, families, companies, and interest groups; but the collected data reveals that small donors (those who give less than $200) are the most effective force in financing elections, while large donors (those who give more than $200) reduces their total percentage in financing the recent elections.

Inside America's Campaign Finance Scandals

There have been instances where candidates or their associates have been accused of soliciting or accepting funds from foreign entities, which is illegal under U.S. election law. For example, during the 2016 presidential campaign, there were allegations of Russian interference in the election, including attempts to funnel money to certain candidates or influence campaign activities through illicit means. Investigations by special counsel Robert Mueller and congressional committees examined these allegations, although conclusive evidence of direct financial involvement was not found.

Pay-to-play schemes involve the exchange of political contributions for access to government officials or favorable treatment in policy decisions. While not always illegal, these arrangements can raise ethical concerns about the influence of money in politics. Scandals involving pay-to-play have implicated politicians at various levels of government, from local officials to members of Congress. One example is the "Bridgegate" scandal in New Jersey, where aides to Governor Chris Christie were convicted of orchestrating lane closures on the George Washington Bridge as political retribution against a mayor who did not endorse Christie's reelection campaign.

The Influence of Campaign Finance on Political Participation

The financing of election campaigns in the United States significantly influences who can participate in political competition, often favoring those with substantial financial backing. The high cost associated with campaigning in the US, including expenses for advertising, staffing, and travel, especially in major national races like the presidency, requires candidates to secure considerable financial resources. This financial demand restricts the pool of potential candidates largely to those who can either self-finance, attract large donations, or achieve substantial media attention.

While the rise of online fundraising platforms has enabled some candidates to rely more on small-dollar donations, democratizing aspects of campaign finance, the overwhelming influence of large donors and PACs persists. This dynamic can lead to a political environment where policymaking is perceived to be heavily influenced by a narrow group of elite donors rather than the broader electorate.

Attempts to create a more level playing field through public financing have been implemented, providing funds to candidates who agree to spending and fundraising limits. However, these programs are not universally available and rarely offer sufficient resources for candidates to compete effectively against well-funded opponents.

As a result, many promising candidates, particularly those from minority, female, or less affluent backgrounds, may be deterred from entering races, thus limiting the diversity of perspectives in government and potentially perpetuating policies that favor affluent and well-connected individuals.

The need for continuous fundraising can distract politicians from governance, potentially leading to policymaking that favors donors over the public interest. The current campaign finance system, therefore, not only influences who can afford to run for office but also impacts the quality of democracy and governance.

Political Campaign Strategies

In U.S. political campaigns, candidates employ diverse strategies to connect with voters and promote their messages. They utilize various spaces, such as rallies, town hall meetings, and digital platforms, to engage with supporters. Typical campaign actions include producing materials like pamphlets and posters, participating in media outreach, and conducting grassroots efforts like door-to-door canvassing. Public appearances, including rallies and community events, allow candidates to interact directly with voters and generate enthusiasm for their campaigns.

Candidates strategically align themselves with individuals and groups to enhance their appeal and reinforce their messages. They often decorate campaign materials and attire with symbols and imagery associated with their political party to visually reinforce their partisan affiliations. Through these efforts, candidates aim to engage voters, mobilize support, and ultimately secure electoral victory.

Media Influence in U.S. Elections

In U.S. elections, the press plays a pivotal role in shaping public opinion and disseminating campaign messages. Candidates actively engage with the media through a variety of channels, including television appearances, press conferences, personal interviews, and digital platforms.

Television shows offer candidates a broad platform to reach diverse audiences and convey their campaign messages. Whether appearing on news programs to discuss policy or talk shows to showcase their personalities, candidates leverage television to connect with voters on both substantive and personal levels.

Press conferences provide candidates with opportunities to address pressing issues, respond to media inquiries, and demonstrate transparency to the public. While these events offer candidates a chance to control the narrative, they also subject them to scrutiny from journalists and the public, requiring adept handling of tough questions and potential controversies.

Additional, personal interviews with newspapers, magazines, radio stations, and online publications allow candidates to delve deeper into their policy positions, share personal anecdotes, and connect with specific audiences. These interviews enable candidates to address issues relevant to particular communities or demographics, showcasing their understanding of diverse perspectives. Overall, the press serves as a vital intermediary between candidates and the electorate, facilitating the exchange of information, shaping public perceptions, and holding candidates accountable. Through active engagement with the media across various platforms, candidates seek to influence public opinion, garner media coverage, and ultimately secure electoral success.

Social Media's Impact

Social media has become a potent tool in U.S. elections, transforming political communication. Candidates leverage platforms like Twitter, Facebook, and Instagram to directly engage voters, share policy proposals, and mobilize support. This immediate and widespread outreach allows candidates to humanize their campaigns and connect with diverse demographics, but it also fosters the spread of misinformation and polarization. The impact on public opinion is profound, influencing voter perceptions and shaping the narrative of the election. While social media enhances citizen engagement, it also poses challenges, such as the manipulation of public opinion and erosion of trust in democratic institutions. Ultimately, its role in strengthening democracy hinges on responsible usage by candidates, voters, and platform providers to foster informed civic discourse and political accountability.

Political Campaigns: Key Do's and Don'ts

In American political campaigns, there are several key "don'ts" for politicians to remember. Firstly, they must avoid any unethical or illegal behavior, such as bribery or fraud, as this can lead to severe consequences. Secondly, making false or misleading statements should be avoided to maintain trust and credibility. Personal attacks on opponents should be avoided, focusing instead on issues rather than individuals. Politicians should actively engage with constituents and voters, as neglecting them can harm their campaign.

Adhering to campaign finance laws is crucial to avoid fines and legal trouble. Furthermore, demonstrating a commitment to diversity and inclusivity is essential in today's political climate.

Social media should be used wisely to prevent posting inappropriate content. Lastly, grassroots campaigning should not be neglected, as building personal connections with voters can greatly impact a campaign's success. Overall, by avoiding these "don'ts" and adhering to ethical standards, politicians can run effective and successful campaigns while maintaining their integrity.

Chapter 6:

Challenges and Opportunities in Governance

Bipartisanship and Unity in Governance

Bipartisanship in the United States means both major political parties, usually the Democrats and Republicans, cooperating to achieve common goals. It's a break from the typical confrontational nature of party politics, where parties often clash over their beliefs.

The Structure of U.S. Government

In the U.S. party system, bipartisanship happens when both parties find agreement and work together on issues. The government has three branches: executive, legislative, and judicial. Apart from the President, the legislative branch includes two parts: the Senate and the House of Representatives.

The Senate has 100 senators, two from each state, regardless of population. They serve six-year terms, with one-third facing election every two years. Senators are elected by their state's voters. The House of Representatives has 435 members, with representation based on each state's population. Representatives serve two-year terms and are elected by voters in their specific districts.

The Legislative Process in the United States

To make a law in the US, a bill is introduced by a member of Congress in either the House or the Senate. It then goes to a committee related to its topic, where it's reviewed, debated, and possibly amended. If the committee approves, the bill moves to the full chamber for debate and vote. If both chambers pass different versions, a committee works to merge them. Once agreed upon, the bill goes to the president, who can sign it into law or veto it. Congress can override a veto with a two-thirds majority in both chambers.

Ensuring Governance

Governability in the US is maintained through checks and balances, separation of powers, and the rule of law. Parties negotiate by finding common ground and making compromises to push their agendas forward. They seek support through persuasion, lobbying, and forming alliances with interest groups. Opposition parties scrutinize and offer alternative proposals, promoting debate and accountability.

Bipartisanship has benefits like promoting cooperation, stability, and problem-solving. However, obstacles such as ideological differences and political games can hinder it. Bipartisanship helps balance powers by fostering cooperation between branches and facilitating legislation. But it can also concentrate power and ignore minority interests.

In summary, bipartisanship is when both major parties work together towards common goals. The U.S. government consists of three branches: executive, legislative, and judicial. Besides the president, the legislative branch includes the Senate and the House of Representatives. To make a law, a bill goes through several steps in Congress before reaching the president. Governability is maintained through checks and balances, and negotiation strategies include finding common ground and building alliances. Bipartisanship has both benefits and obstacles, contributing to the balance of powers but also posing challenges.

Voting Rights in America

Voting is a big deal. It's not just about ticking boxes—it's about being a part of how decisions are made. In the United States, getting the right to vote hasn't been easy. It's been a long journey, with lots of struggles, to make sure everyone can have their say.

Voting is like a badge of citizenship. When you vote, you're not just marking a ballot; you're joining in with everyone else to shape what happens in your country. It's a way of showing that you are part of this community, and that you care about what happens here.

The American Voting Rights Journey

The path to voting rights in the US hasn't been smooth. Different groups, like African Americans, women, and immigrants, had to fight hard to get the right to vote. It wasn't fair—some people were stopped from voting just because of their race, gender, or where they came from. But over time, laws have changed to make sure everyone gets a fair shot at voting. The U.S. Constitution and other laws set out the rules for how voting works and who gets to vote. Here are some important elements:

- **Section 2 of the 14th Amendment (1868)** says that each state should have a fair number of representatives in Congress, based on how many people live there.

- **Section 3 of the 14th Amendment (1868)** talks about what happens if someone tries to overthrow the government—they can't hold public office anymore.

- **The 15th Amendment (1869)** says that nobody can be stopped from voting because of their race, color, or if they used to be enslaved.

- **The 19th Amendment (1920)** gave women the right to vote, making sure they're treated equally in elections.

- **The 22nd Amendment (1951)** limits how long a person can be president to two terms, so there's a changeover and no one person stays in power for too long.

- **The 26th Amendment (1971)** made it so 18-year-olds can vote, recognizing that young adults have a stake in the country's future.

Understanding How U.S. Elections Work

The U.S. electoral process is a multifaceted system encompassing presidential, congressional, state, and local elections. Every four years, the nation undertakes the monumental task of electing a president and vice president. This process begins with primary elections and caucuses held by political parties to select their respective candidates. Subsequently, a general election transpires on the first Tuesday after the first Monday in November, where citizens across the country cast their ballots to determine the next occupants of the White House. However, the popular vote does not directly decide the presidency; rather, an institution known as the Electoral College is tasked with this responsibility.

Comprising representatives from each state, the Electoral College allocates votes based on the state's congressional delegation. The candidate who secures a majority of these electoral votes, specifically 270 out of 538, emerges victorious. While most states operate on a winner-takes-all principle, two states, Maine and Nebraska, distribute electoral votes based on congressional district results.

Simultaneously, the nation also conducts congressional elections, determining the composition of the House of Representatives and the Senate. The House, consisting of 435 members, undergoes a complete renewal every two years. Conversely, the Senate's 100 seats see staggered elections, with one-third up for grabs every two years. This bicameral structure ensures a balance of power within the federal legislature.

State and local elections play a crucial role in American democracy. Governors, state legislators, mayors, city council members, and various other officials are elected to represent the interests of their constituents. These elections, governed by state-specific regulations, contribute to the broader tapestry of governance across the nation.

Integral to the electoral process is voter registration and participation. Citizens must register to vote within their respective states, adhering to specific deadlines and requirements. On Election Day, registered voters exercise their civic duty by casting their ballots either in person at polling stations or via absentee or mail-in voting.

Voter Suppression: Who, How, and Why

Voting is essential for a legitimate government, but not everyone who should be able to vote is allowed to. Over time, the ways and reasons for preventing people from voting have changed.

Who Isn't Allowed to Vote?

In the US, the following groups are typically disqualified from voting:

- Non-citizens: Only citizens can vote in national and most local elections.

- Felons: Many states restrict voting rights for individuals convicted of serious crimes, sometimes extending beyond their sentence.

- Young people under the voting age: The legal voting age is 18.

- People judged mentally incapacitated: Some jurisdictions prevent individuals with significant mental impairments from voting.

Evolution of Voter Suppression

Historically, voter suppression in the US was overt and racially motivated, including tactics like literacy tests and poll taxes designed to disenfranchise African Americans. The Voting Rights Act of 1965 addressed these issues, but suppression tactics have since become subtler, often framed as measures to prevent voter fraud or maintain electoral integrity.

Modern disenfranchisement is often justified by claims of ensuring electoral integrity and preventing fraud. However, critics argue these reasons can be pretexts for suppressing the turnout of groups that might oppose current powers.

Strategies Used to Impede Voting

Suppression tactics can be complex and varied, with some of the most common including:

- **ID Laws:** Requiring specific forms of identification to vote, which can disproportionately affect minorities, the elderly, and low-income citizens who might lack access to such IDs.

- **Voter Purges:** Removing individuals from voting rolls for reasons like inactivity or errors, which can mistakenly disenfranchise eligible voters.

- **Gerrymandering:** Drawing electoral district boundaries to favor one party, undermining the principle of fair representation.

- **Other Methods:** Reducing the number of polling places, limiting early and mail-in voting, and spreading misinformation about voting procedures are other ways voter turnout can be suppressed.

Use and Justification in the US

These suppression methods are actively used and often hotly debated in the United States:

- **ID Laws:** Supporters argue these laws are necessary to prevent impersonation and other types of voter fraud, though such fraud is extremely rare. Opponents contend these laws are unnecessary and disenfranchise vulnerable populations.

- **Voter Purges:** While some say purges are needed to keep voter registries up-to-date, critics argue they often target minority communities and could be motivated by a desire to influence election outcomes.

- **Gerrymandering**: Often defended as a tool for maintaining political advantage, it is criticized for allowing politicians to manipulate electoral outcomes by setting district boundaries that dilute opposition votes.

These tactics can significantly affect voter turnout and election results. For instance, strict ID laws can decrease turnout by 2-3% points, potentially swaying tight races. Between 2014 and 2016, around 16 million voters were purged from the rolls in the US. (United Steel Workers, 2019).

Impact on Democracy and Citizenship

Voter suppression damages democracy by skewing representation and limiting the inclusiveness and fairness of the electoral process. It undermines the foundational democratic principle that governments should derive their power from the consent of the governed, expressed through free and fair elections. This erosion of legitimacy can decrease public trust in government and reduce citizen participation.

When Is Voter Suppression Justifiable?

While defenders of certain suppression tactics claim they are necessary to prevent electoral fraud and ensure the integrity of elections, these arguments are often seen as disproportionate to the actual risks involved. In a democratic society, the goal should be to make voting accessible to all eligible citizens while safeguarding the electoral process against genuine threats, rather than using "integrity" as a pretext for disenfranchising voters.

While it is essential to protect elections from actual fraud and errors, measures implemented to achieve these ends must not inhibit the ability of eligible citizens to vote. Effective democracy requires policies that both secure and facilitate voter participation, reinforcing rather than undermining democratic principles.

The Role of Lobbying and Special Interests

Lobbying is a significant part of American politics, where individuals, groups, or organizations try to influence public policy and lawmakers' decisions. This practice is rooted in the First Amendment of the U.S. Constitution, which guarantees the right to petition the government.

What Is Lobbying?

Lobbyists, as influential representatives of various groups or causes, actively engage in persuasive strategies to sway politicians towards endorsing laws and policies favorable to those they advocate for. Their involvement extends beyond mere persuasion, encompassing essential contributions to crafting and executing policy through the provision of specialized insights, recommendations for legislative alterations, and diligent promotion of distinct advantages sought by their clientele. Their multifaceted roles are instrumental in driving forward the agendas they champion and influencing the trajectory of governmental decisions and actions.

There are mixed views on whether lobbying is a valid form of representation:

- Supporters argue it allows diverse sectors, from businesses to non-profits, to express their interests in a competitive policy environment. They see it as a necessary function in a democracy that values multiple viewpoints.

- Opponents argue that it grants disproportionate influence to the wealthy and well-connected, which can skew public policy away from the common good and undermine democratic values.

Lobbying in Political Processes

Lobbyists wield significant influence in the political arena through various strategic mechanisms. Firstly, they engage in face-to-face meetings with legislators, using these interactions to directly present and advocate for their viewpoints and policy positions. Secondly, lobbyists provide tailored information, including data and research findings, to bolster their causes and guide legislative discussions towards favorable outcomes. Lastly, the controversial practice of campaign contributions also plays a key role, with lobbyists donating funds to political campaigns. This practice triggers debates about the existence of a potentially problematic pay-to-play dynamic, where monetary contributions are perceived as buying influence within the political landscape.

Influential Lobbying Groups

Influential lobbying groups have a significant impact on policy-making decisions. Among these groups:

- **The U.S. Chamber of Commerce:** Advocates for pro-business policies.

- **The National Rifle Association (NRA):** Known for its strong stance on gun rights.

- **The American Medical Association (AMA):** Influences healthcare policy.

- **Pharmaceutical Research and Manufacturers of America (PhRMA):** Significant in shaping drug-related legislation.

Transparency and Regulation

Prioritizing transparency plays a pivotal role in upholding public trust and accountability. In the United States, there are specific legislative measures in place to monitor and oversee lobbying activities. One such important law is the **Lobbying Disclosure Act (LDA)** of 1995, which mandates lobbyists to register and diligently report their activities on a quarterly basis. Moreover, the enactment of the **Honest Leadership and Open Government Act** of 2007 represented a significant step forward by not only increasing the frequency of disclosures but also by implementing more stringent regulations to govern lobbying practices. However, despite these existing regulations, there is an ongoing discourse surrounding whether further reforms are necessary to fortify transparency and fairness in the lobbying landscape. Suggestions for potential enhancements include the imposition of stricter disclosure requirements, implementing real-time reporting mechanisms for lobbyist-legislator interactions, as well as placing limitations on campaign contributions made by lobbyists. Such discussions underscore the continuous efforts being made to uphold the integrity and accountability of lobbying practices in the interest of a transparent and equitable democratic system.

The Role of the Judiciary in Democracy

The judiciary in the United States is a foundational element of the federal government, created to interpret and apply laws. Defined by Article III of the U.S. Constitution, it acts as a check on the legislative and executive branches, ensuring that laws and government actions comply with constitutional principles.

The judiciary's authority is mainly demonstrated through the Supreme Court and lower federal courts. The Supreme Court holds the highest appellate jurisdiction over all federal and state courts on matters of federal law. This structure empowers the judiciary to oversee other government branches via judicial review, established in the pivotal Marbury v. Madison case (1803), which allows courts to invalidate unconstitutional statutes and executive actions.

Stare Decisis, Activism, and Restraint

"Stare decisis," a term signifying "to stand by things decided," serves as the fundamental legal doctrine dictating the adherence to judicial precedent. By upholding this principle, the legal system achieves essential stability and predictability, crucial for the consistent application of the law. Within the realm of the judiciary, two distinct approaches, namely judicial activism and judicial restraint, emerge as contrasting philosophies guiding judicial decisions. Judicial activism involves a proactive stance where courts may make rulings perceived as being influenced by personal or political inclinations rather than strict legal interpretations. Conversely, judicial restraint advocates for a more cautious approach, urging courts to exercise self-restraint and defer to the decisions of other government branches, intervening solely in cases of overt constitutional infringements. These differing approaches highlight the constant tension between judicial interpretation and the broader constitutional framework.

Judicial Structure in the United States

The Supreme Court of the United States is composed of nine justices, which comprises one chief justice and eight associate justices. These justices are appointed by the president of the United States and are subject to confirmation by the Senate. This selection process sets the judiciary apart from other government positions by necessitating approval from a separate branch of government. Such a distinctive method underscores the unique function that the judiciary serves within the framework of governance, reinforcing the principle of checks and balances.

Although justices are appointed by political leaders, specifically the president in the United States, they are expected to uphold the principles of fairness and justice with impartial decisions that are shielded from any form of political pressure because of their lifetime appointments. This unique aspect of judicial independence aims to safeguard the integrity of the legal system by insulating justices from external influences, thereby ensuring that judicial decisions are made solely based on legal principles and constitutional interpretations. Nevertheless, the growing trend of politicizing the appointment process presents significant obstacles to preserving this cherished independence and threatens the fundamental principles upon which the judicial system operates.

The judiciary in the United States is intricately layered with multiple levels of courts overseeing distinct aspects of the legal system. At the apex sits the esteemed Supreme Court, the highest judicial body that interprets the constitution and resolves pivotal legal disputes. Directly beneath are the Circuit Courts of Appeal and District Courts, responsible for handling cases ranging from appeals to original jurisdiction matters at the federal level. The intricate web of state courts diligently manages localized issues governed by state laws, ensuring the effective administration of justice in matters closest to the community. Meanwhile, federal courts meticulously address complex legal matters falling under federal law, such as cases involving interstate disputes and federal entities, embodying the intricate balance of power between state and federal jurisdictions.

The United States Supreme Court, as the highest judicial body in the nation, engages with cases that hold significant national importance, grapple with constitutional matters, or reconcile conflicting legal interpretations from lower courts. These cases find their way to the Supreme Court through writs of certiorari, a formal process where the Court exercises its discretion in selecting cases for review. Emblematic cases such as Brown v. Board of Education (1954), a landmark decision that put an end to racial segregation in public schools, and Roe v. Wade (1973), which recognized a woman's right to seek an abortion, underscore the pivotal role the Court plays in shaping the broader societal fabric through its adjudications.

Constitutional Provisions

Article III of the U.S. Constitution establishes the federal judiciary, defining the powers and jurisdiction of federal courts, including the Supreme Court. It grants federal courts the authority of judicial review, allowing them to interpret laws and the Constitution and to check the actions of the legislative and executive branches. The 10th Amendment reinforces the principle of federalism by reserving powers not delegated to the federal government to the states or the people. It emphasizes the limited nature of federal authority and grants states substantial autonomy in governance. Together, Article III and the Tenth Amendment form the framework for the American system of government, delineating the roles and powers of the federal judiciary and ensuring a balance between federal and state authority.

Governance and Environmental Sustainability

U.S. governance comprises the decision-making and actions taken by federal, state, and local governments aimed at promoting the common good. The goal is to create favorable living conditions for most of the population, recognizing that it's impossible to satisfy everyone equally in a democracy. This system tries to balance individual rights with the well-being of the community.

Sustainability means using natural resources wisely to meet today's needs without harming future generations' ability to meet their own needs. It's about ensuring long-term environmental health and social equity.

US Environmental Challenges and Responses

The world faces significant environmental challenges like global warming and climate change, which include rising temperatures, melting ice caps, and more extreme weather events. Most scientists agree these issues are driven by human activities, although some skeptics question the severity or causes of these changes. Those in favor of this view cite extensive data showing a trend of climatic changes, while critics often bring up economic concerns or contradictory evidence.

The United States deals with various environmental problems, such as floods, heat waves, and extreme cold events. These not only disrupt ecosystems but also affect human safety and property, leading to significant economic and health-related costs.

Environmental policies often conflict with short-term economic interests, leading to political disagreements and slow legislative progress. Over the years, laws like the Clean Air Act and the Clean Water Act have helped reduce pollution. Efforts such as the US' participation in the Paris Agreement under the Obama administration (later withdrawn by Trump and rejoined by Biden) show the fluctuating commitment to tackling climate change.

Environmental Goals vs. Economic Realities

Recently, ambitious environmental proposals like the Green New Deal have ignited debates. Supporters believe it's crucial for addressing climate change and economic disparities, but opponents worry about its cost and practicality. Many progressive environmental proposals face hurdles in Congress, reflecting deep political divisions and economic concerns from various groups.

In summary, balancing environmental sustainability with economic growth and social stability is a complex challenge for U.S. policymakers, fraught with conflicts between long-term environmental goals and immediate economic interests.

The Art of Political Compromise

Reaching new agreements for the common good in a society involves strategies from both citizens and government, inspired by the ancient

Greek concept of politics as communal ethics. This concept sees every citizen as crucial to the community's welfare, a practice that aligns individual virtue with the collective benefit.

Empowering Democracy: Citizen Engagement for Progress

Governments can create opportunities for public engagement through town hall meetings, consultations, and online feedback platforms. These initiatives allow citizens to express their views and contribute ideas, promoting a sense of shared responsibility and community. Citizens can enhance their participation by staying informed, voting, joining public discussions, or volunteering. Educational programs about civic duties can further empower citizens, enabling them to effectively engage in community and political dialogues.

Methods such as bipartisan committees, negotiations, and compromise are essential. Political actors can work across party lines on common issues like healthcare and environmental protection, focusing on mutual interests rather than differences.

Practical approaches include adopting structured negotiation frameworks that require good faith participation or utilizing neutral mediators for resolving disputes. Such methods hinge on a mutual commitment to honest dialogue and shared objectives.

The Political Balancing Act

In any democratic society, the tension between diverse individual interests and collective goals is inherent. Individuals naturally prioritize their personal interests, which can sometimes conflict with the broader goals of the community. Politics serves as the mechanism to navigate this tension, ensuring that the needs and desires of diverse groups are considered while advancing the common good.

By engaging in political processes such as dialogue, negotiation, and compromise, conflicting interests can be reconciled to prevent violence and reduce social conflict. Through democratic institutions like elections, legislative bodies, and public forums, individuals have avenues to express their concerns and advocate for their interests within the framework of collective decision-making.

Moreover, politics plays a crucial role in establishing priorities and seeking enduring solutions to societal challenges. It provides a platform for deliberation and consensus-building, allowing for the formulation of policies that address the needs of the many while respecting the rights of the few. Through effective governance and policy implementation, politics fosters social cohesion and stability by promoting fairness, justice, and inclusivity.

Politics is the art of balancing diverse perspectives and interests to achieve common objectives. It serves as a vital tool for maintaining harmony and progress in democratic societies, ensuring that the voices of all citizens are heard and their aspirations are represented in the pursuit of a better future.

The Future of American Democracy

America's democratic landscape is fraught with pressing issues, threatening the core of its political identity. From climate change to immigration, globalization to inequality, these challenges demand attention and action. Let's explore them backed by real-world examples.

Environmental Challenges

Climate change, a pressing global issue, has dire consequences, such as the increasing severity of wildfires in the Western regions, highlighting the urgent need for action. As we observe these devastating effects, it becomes essential to prioritize finding solutions that allow us to generate income while also addressing environmental concerns to ensure a sustainable future for our planet and future generations.

Immigration

The ongoing debate surrounding immigration policies and border control is undeniably significant. Within this contentious issue, the focus often gravitates towards the influx of individuals seeking entry at the southern border. Opinions vary widely on how to address this complex challenge—from calls for stricter enforcement to proposals advocating for increased support and assistance for these migrants. Navigating through these contrasting perspectives and finding a balanced solution proves to be a daunting task in a situation that is rife with social, political, and humanitarian implications.

Globalization and Global Order

Trade tensions with powerful nations like China and conflicts erupting in distant regions are just some issues arising from our interdependence. Striking a delicate balance between fostering harmony with all mankind while safeguarding our own interests emerges as a pressing necessity in our quest to navigate these intricacies of a closely woven global community.

Cultural Integration/ Differentiation

America is undoubtedly a melting pot of diverse individuals and cultures, each bringing a unique tapestry to the collective landscape. It is not uncommon for clashes to arise on issues concerning acceptance and appropriateness. Topics such as the appropriation of cultural symbols and the language domain can often spark disagreements. Despite these potential conflicts, it is paramount that we approach these differences with a sense of mutual respect and understanding.

Inequalities

Stark disparities in wealth distribution became more evident—a stark contrast emerged between those who have abundant financial resources and those who struggle to make ends meet, with people of color disproportionately affected. This period shed light on the deep-rooted inequalities that persist in our society, emphasizing the urgency for creating equal opportunities for all individuals to thrive and access a decent standard of living.

Disinformation and Misinformation

It's a common occurrence to come across false information online, which can be significantly damaging. Instances where misinformation is intentionally spread, especially regarding important topics such as elections or vaccines, pose a serious threat to public trust and understanding.

Technological Advances and New Ethics Debates

Technology is undoubtedly fascinating and has brought forth numerous advancements, but at the same time, it can evoke feelings of apprehension and concern. Innovations, such as robots and surveillance technologies, have prompted discussions surrounding privacy and ethical considerations. As we navigate this rapidly evolving landscape, it becomes imperative to establish clear guidelines and regulations to safeguard individual rights and ensure the security of our personal information in a fair and transparent manner.

Political Polarization

People are deeply fractured when it comes to political views, polarized into opposing factions as if competing in a fierce game where consensus seems unattainable. The shocking incident of certain individuals storming the capitol vividly illustrates the detrimental consequences of our inability to engage in meaningful dialogue and find common ground. It is imperative that we actively seek pathways to collaboration and understanding, fostering a spirit of unity even amidst disagreement.

Citizens' Indifference and Lack of Participation

Many individuals across various demographics tend to show disinterest or indifference towards political matters. This disengagement often stems from the misconception that politics has no direct impact on their lives or that their individual actions wouldn't bring about any significant change. However, it is crucial to emphasize that every person's perspective and participation hold immense value in shaping the course of governance and societal decision-making. Encouraging a higher voter turnout and fostering a culture where diverse voices are heard and valued becomes imperative for creating a more inclusive and participatory democracy.

Chapter 7:

The Power of Political Engagement

In this chapter, we explore a transformative journey delving deep into the essence of democracy. This unique narrative challenges traditional perspectives by highlighting the intrinsic value of grassroots activism and civic engagement as driving forces behind political evolution. Rather than fixating solely on governmental structures, our focus shifts to illuminate the dynamic relationship between civil society and governance. By illustrating how everyday individuals can wield significant influence, we reveal the lasting impact of community mobilization, advocacy efforts, and social campaigns in shaping policy directions and nurturing inclusive decision-making mechanisms.

Political Movements and Contemporary Democracy

Politics isn't just for politicians—it's for everyone. Aristotle called humans "zoon politikon," highlighting our natural inclination to engage in collective decision-making.

Political Movements

Political movements are organized efforts to bring about social, economic, or ideological change. They gain strength through widespread support, clear messaging, and strategic actions.

Let's look at some historical examples:

- **The Temperance Movement:** This movement, starting in the 19th century, aimed to reduce alcohol consumption, seeing it as a cause of societal problems like poverty and crime. Advocates pushed for laws restricting or banning alcohol sales, leading to Prohibition in the U.S. in the 1920s. Though Prohibition was later repealed due to issues like non-compliance, the Temperance Movement shifted public attitudes towards alcohol and influenced future policies.

- **The Feminist Movement for Suffrage:** In the late 19th and early 20th centuries, the feminist movement fought for women's right to vote. Through marches, petitions, and civil disobedience, suffragists challenged patriarchal systems. Their efforts led to the Nineteenth Amendment in 1920, granting women the right to vote and marking a significant step towards gender equality.

- **The Civil Rights Movement:** Emerging in the 1950s and 1960s, this movement aimed at combatting racial injustice and segregation. Led by figures like Martin Luther King Jr., activists used nonviolent tactics, such as sit-ins and boycotts, to challenge discriminatory laws. Their actions resulted in landmark legislation like the Civil Rights Act of 1964 and the Voting Rights Act of 1965, which outlawed segregation and protected voting rights for minorities.

Political movements play a crucial role in democracy by amplifying marginalized voices and holding elected officials accountable. However, they can also create tensions with established institutions and electoral processes.

While formal channels provide avenues for participation, they may not always address the needs of marginalized groups, leading people to mobilize outside traditional frameworks for change.

Youth Movements and Political Change

Youth movements have been pivotal in sparking political change because of their dynamism, idealism, and readiness to question norms. Historically, these movements have significantly impacted societal attitudes and policies.

Historical Youth Movements

Historical youth movements in the United States have been pivotal in driving significant social and political changes. During the 1950s and 1960s, the Civil Rights Movement saw youth like those in the Student Nonviolent Coordinating Committee leading efforts against racial segregation, highlighted by events such as the Birmingham Children's Crusade. The 1960s and 1970s also witnessed the Anti-Vietnam War Movement, where student protests against the draft marked major campus unrest, notably culminating in the tragic Kent State shootings.

The Free Speech Movement in 1964 at UC Berkeley set precedents for student activism on free speech and academic freedom. Environmental awareness was galvanized by the establishment of Earth Day in 1970, largely driven by student activists, leading to impactful environmental legislation. The Women's Rights Movement and the LGBTQ+ Rights Movement also saw significant contributions from young people, pushing for gender equality and LGBTQ+ rights through various forms of advocacy, including the formation of campus groups like Gay-Straight Alliances.

Current Youth Movements

Current youth movements are dynamic forces advocating for substantial changes across environmental, social, and educational spheres:

- Climate Activism is a major focus, with urgent efforts to address climate change, enforce carbon emission reductions, and enhance renewable energy adoption. Prominent figures like Greta Thunberg have spearheaded global climate strikes, significantly raising awareness and impacting international policies, such as the Paris Agreement, although implementation challenges persist.

- Social Justice Movements, such as Black Lives Matter, address systemic racism, police brutality, and advocate for racial justice and policing reforms. Founded by Alicia Garza, Patrisse Cullors, and Opal Tometi, these movements employ protests, community organizing, and advocacy to drive change. They have ignited critical discussions and prompted some reforms in racial and policing issues, although continuous efforts are required to overcome persistent challenges.

- Student Activism focuses on making education affordable, alleviating student debt, and promoting diversity on campuses. Notable advocates like Emma González and David Hogg rose to prominence after the Parkland school shooting, pushing for gun control and educational reforms through rallies, walkouts, and advocacy. These efforts have influenced policy discussions and brought about changes in gun control laws and educational policies.

Together, these movements illustrate the powerful influence of youth activism in shaping policy and reforming practices across various sectors, demonstrating a relentless pursuit of justice and sustainability.

U.S. Political Responses to Youth Activism

U.S. political institutions have varied responses to youth movements, generally falling into three categories: repression, co-option, and reform. Historically, movements challenging the status quo, like the Civil Rights and Anti-Vietnam War protests, often faced initial repression, exemplified by police brutality and incidents like the Kent State shootings. Co-option occurs as political parties attempt to dilute the impact of movements by adopting their rhetoric without implementing substantial changes, often to attract young voters.

However, when youth movements garner significant public support and political leverage, they can lead to genuine reforms. Notable successes include the Civil Rights Act of 1964 and recent police reforms influenced by the Black Lives Matter movement. Overall, while responses can include attempts to suppress or superficially adopt movement goals, sustained activism has the potential to achieve meaningful policy changes.

The Art of Civil Discourse

Civil discourse is the bedrock of democratic societies, enabling respectful and constructive communication, even amid disagreements. It involves engaging in dialogue while upholding values like tolerance, respect, empathy, and active listening. Civil discourse fosters an environment where diverse opinions can coexist, and disagreements are approached with a commitment to understanding and finding common ground.

Active listening is crucial in civil discourse, requiring genuinely hearing and understanding others' perspectives without immediately countering. This fosters deeper understanding and meaningful exchanges. Tolerance is essential, recognizing the importance of diverse thought and accepting that others may hold different opinions, even if strongly disagreed with. Respect means treating others with dignity and courtesy, refraining from personal attacks, and focusing on the substance of the argument.

Empathy plays a key role, allowing individuals to understand others' perspectives deeply and bridge divides. Constructive arguments supported by evidence and reason are vital, promoting reasoned debate over emotional appeals or personal attacks.

However, civil discourse has limits, particularly regarding hate speech. While freedom of speech is fundamental, it does not extend to speech promoting violence, discrimination, or hatred based on factors like race, ethnicity, religion, gender, or sexual orientation. Hate speech undermines civil discourse and poses a threat to marginalized communities.

In democracies, civil discourse navigates the tension between majority rule and minority representation. While majority rule is essential, protections for minority rights are crucial. Civil discourse ensures minority voices are heard and respected, even in the face of majority opposition.

Challenges to civil discourse include echo chambers and filter bubbles in both traditional and virtual public spheres. Social media platforms amplify extreme voices and misinformation, hindering meaningful dialogue.

Despite challenges, civil discourse is vital for democracy. It promotes understanding, tolerance, and respect, fostering an inclusive society where diverse voices are valued. It strengthens democratic institutions, promotes civic engagement, and leads to better decision-making.

To promote civil discourse, political leaders can lead by example, educators can teach critical thinking skills and media literacy, and civil society organizations can facilitate dialogue across diverse communities.

Civil discourse is essential for democracy's health. By upholding values like active listening, tolerance, respect, empathy, and constructive argumentation, we create a more inclusive society where all voices are valued and heard.

Community Organizing and Grassroots Campaigns

The Tale of Accountability and Civic Engagement

In the British paradigm, accountability underscores the responsibility of government officials to act in the best interest of the public, with citizens holding them answerable for their actions. This concept emphasizes the reciprocal relationship between government and citizens, where the latter plays an active role in governance. As active members of their own government, citizens engage in civil discourse, participate in elections, and advocate for their interests through grassroots organizing. By holding leaders accountable and actively shaping policies, citizens ensure the government remains responsive to the needs and aspirations of the people it serves.

In early U.S. history, grassroots politics found its origins in colonial times when communities came together to collectively tackle shared obstacles and champion their concerns. Emanating from the grassroots level, initiatives such as town hall assemblies and protests opposing unjust governmental actions underscored the deep-rooted tradition of civic participation and communal mobilization exhibited by the American populace.

This robust participation not only served as a cornerstone for democracy but, more significantly, as a means of empowering individuals to shape their own futures and guaranteeing that their viewpoints resonated throughout society.

Throughout American history, civil engagement and community organization have stood as pillars of democracy, serving as vital instruments for societal progress. By fostering unity among individuals, they provide a platform to collectively address common issues, strengthen social bonds, and ensure governmental transparency.

Examples of grassroots movements are widespread in daily life, with local associations tackling various matters such as crime prevention and improving infrastructure, while advocacy groups passionately rally support for causes like environmental sustainability and equal social rights. Through acts of volunteerism, activism, and active civic involvement, communities consistently exhibit their capacity to mobilize and drive positive transformation starting from the grassroots level.

Tension and Cooperation Between Community Organizing and Government

The relationship between community organizing and government power is characterized by a complex interplay of dynamics that requires finesse to navigate effectively. While community organizing plays a pivotal role in ensuring transparency and accountability within government structures by acting as a vigilant watchdog and a voice for the marginalized, it also seeks to collaboratively engage with authorities when mutual goals align. This duality fosters a cyclical relationship of push and pull, where grassroots movements challenge the status quo by mobilizing citizens to challenge existing policies and demand change. By leveraging a combination of peaceful protests, educational campaigns, and grassroots initiatives, community organizers strive to bridge the gap between the governed and the governing, fostering a system that is responsive and inclusive.

This activism can sometimes lead to tension as government officials may view grassroots movements as challenging their authority or disrupting the status quo. Conflicts may arise when government actions are perceived as infringing upon the rights or well-being of the community, leading to resistance and pushback from organized citizens. Consequently, these clashes between the grassroots movements advocating for change and the government striving to maintain control can escalate, sparking debates, protests, and even legal battles.

While tension between community organizing and government power is inherent in the democratic process, establishing collaboration and constructive relationships can be pivotal in driving more efficient governance and fostering favorable outcomes for communities. It is essential to foster mutual understanding and cultivate open communication channels between grassroots organizers and government authorities in order to effectively manage and enhance this intricate dynamic. By actively seeking common interests and promoting meaningful dialogue, both parties can work together to address challenges, leverage strengths, and ultimately create sustainable solutions that benefit society as a whole.

The Influence of Grassroots Movements in American Society

Grassroots campaigns in the USA are powerful movements that emerge from the bottom up, driven by the passion and dedication of ordinary citizens seeking to enact change. These campaigns often tackle a wide range of social, political, and environmental issues, employing diverse strategies to mobilize support, raise awareness, and influence policy.

One of the most notable examples is the **Civil Rights Movement**, which challenged racial segregation and discrimination through nonviolent protests, marches, and community organizing. Leaders like Martin Luther King Jr. mobilized communities, while volunteers coordinated logistics and legal support. The movement's efforts culminated in landmark legislation, such as the Civil Rights Act of 1964 and the Voting Rights Act of 1965, significantly advancing civil rights for African Americans.

Similarly, the **Occupy Wall Street Movement** emerged in response to economic inequality and corporate influence on politics. Organizers utilized protests, social media, and public occupations to raise awareness and spark discussions about wealth disparity. While the movement did not achieve specific policy changes, it succeeded in highlighting issues of income inequality and corporate power, igniting a broader conversation about economic justice.

The **Women's March**, beginning in 2017, mobilized millions of people across the USA and globally to advocate for women's rights and social justice. Organizers coordinated massive demonstrations in cities, requiring funding for permits, security, and logistics. The march galvanized support for issues such as reproductive rights, gender equality, and sexual harassment, serving as a catalyst for ongoing activism and political engagement.

Environmental grassroots movements, exemplified by organizations like the **Sierra Club** and **Greenpeace**, employ a variety of tactics to advocate for environmental protection and sustainability. These movements engage in public education, lobbying, litigation, and direct action to raise awareness and influence policy. Over the years, they have played a significant role in shaping environmental policies, regulations, and public opinion, leading to the establishment of protected areas, pollution controls, and renewable energy initiatives.

In all these examples, grassroots campaigns rely on the energy and dedication of ordinary citizens coming together to address pressing issues. They require strong leadership, community mobilization, funding, legal support, and media attention to succeed. While outcomes vary, grassroots movements have proven to be powerful forces for social change, driving progress and advancing the causes they champion.

Digital Activism and Social Media Influence

Social Media: Benefits and Challenges

In the past two decades, technological advancements have dramatically reshaped every aspect of our lives, making social media an integral component of modern society. Social media's influence extends from shaping popular culture to impacting political landscapes, generating economic value, and affecting individuals on deep social and psychological levels.

Despite extensive research and numerous proposals on how individuals should interact with social media healthily, consensus remains elusive. Social media offers significant benefits, such as instant connectivity across cultures and geographies, but it also poses severe challenges, including mental health issues and the spread of misinformation.

Social Media's Political Impact in the US

In the United States, the intertwining of social media and politics has become increasingly evident, particularly highlighted during the 2016 elections and the COVID-19 pandemic. U.S. intelligence confirmed

Russian interference in the 2016 election, which former President Trump interpreted as a challenge to his presidency's legitimacy. This event marked a shift where social media's role in information and disinformation campaigns garnered focused attention from both intelligence services and the state.

The pandemic further complicated social media's role in politics, with platforms becoming battlegrounds for misinformation regarding vaccines and virus origins. This led to intense conflicts between the Biden administration and social media companies, with conservative critics accusing the administration of infringing on free speech through efforts to curb harmful misinformation.

Concerns have also grown around the immense data control exercised by tech giants like Google, Facebook, and Twitter. Accusations of monopolistic practices have been voiced by some Democratic leaders, while Europe has taken regulatory actions against these companies. However, the U.S. government has generally chosen cooperation over confrontation, recognizing these companies' significant contributions to the economy and their extensive lobbying efforts.

Social Media Censorship: Legal Battles and Free Speech

The debate extends to accusations from conservative Republicans that the Biden administration misuses antitrust laws to suppress conservative viewpoints on social media—allegations that highlight ongoing tensions over content censorship. The administration counters that its actions aim to ensure public access to accurate information and protect public health without unfairly targeting specific groups.

These controversies have led to legal challenges, including a notable case where a Trump-appointed judge signaled intentions to rule against the Biden administration for allegedly infringing on free speech by influencing social media platform policies. The case, which hinges on complex freedom of expression issues, appears poised to escalate to the Supreme Court.

Navigating the Political Landscape

In the daily grind of a typical worker—let's call her Emma—her day begins with an alarm at 6:30 a.m. She quickly grabs a coffee and joins the rush of commuters, spending over an hour to reach her office. Her workday is packed with meetings and deadlines. By evening, after reversing her morning commute, Emma is drained. Cooking dinner, helping her kids with homework, and a brief unwind in front of the TV round off her day before she collapses into bed. Finding time and energy for politics might seem impossible in Emma's packed schedule, with her days already overflowing with commitments. However, it is crucial for her to recognize that political decisions have a far-reaching impact, influencing everything from her morning coffee to her bedtime routine.

The quality of the roads, the safety of her bus ride, and the efficiency of her city's traffic management are all intricately intertwined with the political decisions made by governing bodies. These decisions guide the allocation of resources and funding, impacting the maintenance of infrastructure and the implementation of safety measures that directly affect her daily commute and overall well-being. Beyond this immediate impact, the taxes deducted from her paycheck further underscore the interconnectedness of her financial contribution to public services that play a vital role in her life—from shaping the educational experience of her children in schools to ensuring access to crucial healthcare services in hospitals they may need.

The ongoing discussions surrounding retirement age and Social Security benefits have become significant focal points in current political discourse. These conversations are not merely theoretical discussions; rather, they represent crucial determinations made by elected representatives that will profoundly shape Emma's lifestyle and financial security during her later years. It is essential for policymakers to carefully consider the implications of their decisions on individuals like Emma, as these choices carry lasting ramifications.

What Steps Can Emma Take to Influence the Political Decisions That Affect Her Life?

Emma has several available strategies to influence her community and government while accommodating her busy schedule:

- She can vote to select leaders who shape crucial policies like retirement and infrastructure.

- Attending community meetings enables her to stay abreast of local developments and contribute to neighborhood discussions, fitting these into her evenings or weekends.

- Joining advocacy groups allows her to support causes like public transport and retirement age with minimal time commitment yet significant effect.

- Emma can also use social media and online platforms to voice her opinions and support various causes efficiently whenever she has free time.

- Staying informed through news podcasts during commutes or reading summaries helps her understand policy impacts.

- Volunteering for political campaigns provides a direct way to influence specific issues or candidates she supports.

Together, these activities empower Emma to be an active participant in her democracy with flexibility and efficiency.

The Power of One Vote

In democratic societies where the right to vote stands as a foundational cornerstone of civil liberties, it is a prevailing misconception among many individual voters that their single vote might not hold significant weight in the grand scheme of political decision-making processes, particularly in the midst of rambunctious campaign noise and heated debates. The often disenchanting sentiment, fueled by feelings of disillusionment or indifference, revolves around the notion that "just one vote won't make a difference" or the belief that "nobody really cares about my vote" while sometimes stemming from a lack of enthusiasm towards any of the candidates running for office. However, it is vital to recognize that each vote cast, no matter how solitary it may seem, carries with it a profound influence and unparalleled power when it comes to shaping the outcomes of elections, and thus, the direction of the society at large.

My Vote Won't Decide Anything

The belief that one vote does not matter is a significant misconception that is disproven time and time again by various historical instances. Throughout history, there have been countless examples where the impact of a singular vote has reverberated significantly. Take, for example, the pivotal moment in 1876, when a mere single vote in the Electoral College determined the presidency in favor of Rutherford B. Hayes.

This demonstration of the power of a single ballot extends into more recent times, with local elections, including those for town council seats and school board positions, often hinging on just a handful of votes. In such instances, it becomes clear that not only does each vote hold weight, but it can also be the deciding factor that shapes the course of governance and representation at the local level.

Additionally, when individuals choose not to participate in the voting process, they effectively relinquish their influence on crucial decisions to a potentially limited subset of voters. This shift in decision-making dynamics may result in the election of officials who may not accurately or fully represent the diverse perspectives and preferences of the overall population, ultimately impacting the alignment of governance with the collective desires of society as a whole.

It is Just One Vote. Nobody Cares

Another viewpoint underscores a sense of isolation from the political process, a feeling that the system does not value the individual's input. However, democracy is fundamentally built on the principle of individual voices collectively shaping the nation's future. Each vote is a signal, a piece of feedback to policymakers about public preferences and priorities. When people choose to vote, they are effectively saying that they do have a stake in societal outcomes and that their concerns merit attention.

I Don't Like Any of the Candidates

The dissatisfaction among voters regarding the available candidates stands as a legitimate concern, prompting a call for the democratic system to adapt and refine itself. Nevertheless, refraining from voting does not serve as an effective mode of protest; rather, it represents a passive forfeiture of one's ability to exert influence. Opting instead to support a lesser-known or third-party candidate, or engaging in a write-in candidacy, offers avenues for voters to express their discontent while actively participating in the electoral process. These actions serve as clear messages to major political parties, signaling the imperative for them to nominate candidates who more authentically reflect the sentiments of the electorate.

The Power of Voting in Democracy

Active participation of citizens is vital for a strong democracy. Voting is not just a right; it's a civic duty that sustains democratic health. Each vote adds to governance's legitimacy and stability, ensuring that the government represents society's diverse needs and aspirations.

Voting goes beyond elections, influencing policy decisions affecting daily life, from education to healthcare. Participating in elections grants citizens a direct say in policy implementation and resource allocation. Citizens' engagement through voting shapes the course of governance, making it more responsive to societal demands and fostering a vibrant democratic system.

The Responsibility of Democratic Citizenship

Every right comes with a duty. The right to vote, a cornerstone of democracy, carries the responsibility of active participation in the democratic process. This responsibility transcends the simple act of casting a ballot; it encompasses staying informed, engaging in discourse, holding elected officials accountable, and even considering running for office.

Individual actions can yield collective impacts. By recognizing the power of their rights and choosing to exercise them, people contribute to building a more engaged and informed community. Informed citizens are better equipped to address challenges and seize opportunities, both locally and nationally. Thus, participation in democracy extends far beyond the ballot box—it is an ongoing commitment to shaping the future.

Living in a democratic society offers a multitude of benefits. These include freedoms of expression, assembly, and religion, as well as protection under the law. Moreover, citizens can influence government action through their participation. These benefits are not merely coincidental; they are the result of generations of active and engaged citizenship. Participation in democracy is not just a privilege; it is a reciprocal responsibility. Engaging in the electoral process is one of the most direct ways individuals can shape the society in which they live. By exercising their right to vote and actively participating in civic life, citizens uphold their end of the social contract, contributing to the preservation and strengthening of democracy.

In conclusion, the responsibility of democratic citizenship goes beyond merely exercising the right to vote. It encompasses active participation, informed engagement, and a commitment to shaping the future of society. By recognizing the importance of their rights and responsibilities, citizens play a vital role in preserving and strengthening democracy for generations to come.

Chapter 8:

Navigating Political Discourse and Media

The Era of Fake News and Misinformation

From its inception with Gutenberg's printing press in the 15th century, mass communication has continually evolved. Newspapers and pamphlets emerged as influential mediums, shaping public opinion.

The 20th century witnessed the rise of broadcast media, including radio and television, offering real-time news and entertainment to vast audiences. Politicians seized upon these platforms for propaganda, directly reaching millions of households.

As technology advanced, cable television emerged in the late 20th century, ushering in round-the-clock news coverage. Political campaigns adapted, relying heavily on television advertising to sway voters.

Then came the internet, transforming mass media entirely. Instant global communication became possible, and digital platforms like Facebook and Twitter emerged, revolutionizing the dissemination and consumption of information.

Influence of Mass Media on Politics: Tactics and Strategies

Throughout history, political actors have leveraged mass media to shape public opinion and sway electoral outcomes. Their tactics include:

- **Propaganda:** Governments and political parties spread biased or misleading information to advance their agendas and undermine opponents.

- **Advertising:** Political campaigns allocate significant resources to advertising on both traditional and digital media platforms, aiming to influence voter perceptions.

- **Spin:** Politicians and their representatives strategically craft narratives during media appearances to frame events favorably and shape public discourse.

Democracy's Double-Edged Sword

The emergence of digital media brings forth a dual impact on the human right to access and express information. On one hand, digital media democratizes access to information, empowering individuals to engage in public discourse and demand accountability from those in power.

On the other hand, the widespread dissemination of fake news, misinformation, and disinformation poses a significant challenge. It erodes the public's capacity to distinguish between truth and falsehood, thereby jeopardizing the integrity of democratic processes.

Fake News and Political Influence

Fake news, or false and misleading information presented as genuine news, serves as a potent political tool. It influences elections by disseminating false narratives about candidates or issues, swaying public opinion and impacting electoral results. Additionally, fake news undermines trust in mainstream media and democratic institutions, fostering an environment conducive to authoritarianism.

In the past, newspapers fabricated stories to boost sales or further specific agendas, such as the New York Sun's 1835 "Great Moon Hoax," falsely claiming the discovery of life on the moon. In modern times, during the 2016 U.S. presidential election, fabricated news stories circulated widely on social media, influencing voter perceptions. For example, false reports about Hillary Clinton's health and alleged criminal activities gained traction online.

Furthermore, misinformation, which entails spreading false or misleading information unintentionally, and disinformation, involving the deliberate spread of falsehoods to deceive or manipulate, proliferated during the COVID-19 pandemic. This abundance of false information led to confusion and distrust in public health measures, exacerbating the global crisis.

Threats to Democracy

The proliferation of fake news, misinformation, and disinformation poses a significant threat to democracy by distorting public debate and hindering informed decision-making. False information undermines civil discourse, making it challenging to engage in rational debate and find common ground.

Moreover, when individuals are bombarded with falsehoods, they struggle to make informed choices, which undermines the functioning of democratic institutions.

The evolution of mass media has both empowered public engagement and presented challenges to democracy. The prevalence of fake news, misinformation, and disinformation threatens the integrity of democratic processes, highlighting the critical importance of media literacy and critical thinking in the digital age.

Media Literacy and Critical Thinking

In today's digital age, the role of a communicator in mass or social media has significantly evolved beyond being limited to trained journalists or media professionals. Nowadays, nearly anyone with access to the internet and various social media platforms has the power to share information and influence audiences. In contrast to traditional journalism, the digital sphere imposes no formal prerequisites for individuals who wish to communicate information. However, there are certain implicit standards that individuals are expected to uphold, which include demonstrating a sufficient level of literacy and possessing the critical skills necessary to assess the credibility, importance, precision, clarity, and objectivity of the information they choose to disseminate to their audience. This shift in communication dynamics emphasizes the need for communicators in the digital realm to not only be proficient in utilizing different platforms but also to understand the responsibilities that come with wielding the power to shape narratives and inform the public.

Traditional Media and Fulfillment of Requirements

While traditional media outlets often strive to meet these expectations, not all of them consistently fulfill these requirements. Despite having trained journalists and established editorial processes, traditional media can still fall short in terms of reliability, relevance, accuracy, transparency, and impartiality. Bias, sensationalism, and commercial interests can sometimes overshadow the pursuit of objective reporting. Moreover, traditional media may not always offer diverse perspectives, leading to a limited understanding of complex issues among audiences. It is crucial for media organizations to continuously evaluate and improve their practices to address these shortcomings. Emphasizing ethical guidelines, fact-checking protocols, and a commitment to presenting diverse viewpoints are essential steps in ensuring that traditional media fulfills its role as an informer of the public. By prioritizing accuracy over speed and cultivating a culture of transparency and accountability, media outlets can regain trust and credibility with their audiences.

Diverse Perspectives in the Digital Era

It's really important to show different points of view to people. This helps them make up their own minds by considering lots of different ideas. When we see things from different angles, we become better at thinking critically and understanding issues more deeply. Social media lets lots of different voices be heard, which makes discussions more interesting and thoughtful. But sometimes, there's so much information out there that it's hard to tell what's true and what's not, especially when people only listen to ideas they already agree with. So, while diversity of perspectives is great, we also need to be careful about misinformation and not just stick to our own little bubbles.

Journalism's Impartiality Challenge

Although the quest for impartiality is a cornerstone of journalism, achieving absolute objectivity can prove to be a challenging endeavor. It is intrinsic to recognize that each individual's viewpoints and narratives are inherently tinted by personal biases, molded through a kaleidoscope of past experiences, cultural backgrounds, and deeply ingrained beliefs. Moreover, the operational ethos of media establishments can be significantly swayed by external factors such as corporate affiliations or political alignments, profoundly influencing the editorial trajectory they embark on. Nevertheless, amidst these formidable hurdles, journalists are tasked with the profound responsibility of steadfastly upholding principles of fairness and equilibrium by meticulously presenting a spectrum of perspectives, rigorously validating the veracity of facts, and dutifully disclosing any potential conflicts of interest that may arise in the course of their reportage.

Being ethical with information means being honest, acting with integrity, and being accountable. Journalists need to tell the truth accurately and make sure their work isn't misleading. They should also be transparent by sharing any conflicts of interest or biases they might have. It's important for journalists to respect people's privacy and dignity in their stories, avoiding sensationalism or using them just to get attention.

The democratization of media in today's digital age has significantly broadened the landscape of communicators, facilitating the ease with which individuals, irrespective of geographical boundaries, can now disseminate information and engage with diverse audiences. While the traditional media sector strives to uphold standards of reliability, accuracy, transparency, and impartiality, there are instances where inherent biases, commercial pressures, or editorial choices may inadvertently hinder the delivery of unbiased and objective content. It has become increasingly evident that the provision of a wide array of perspectives to viewers and readers alike plays an integral role in nurturing critical thinking skills and fostering a society that is well-informed and cognizant of various viewpoints. Acknowledging the inherent challenge of complete impartiality in reporting, journalists are encouraged to actively pursue fairness and equilibrium in their work by presenting a balanced array of opinions and abiding by ethical guidelines that underscore the values of truthfulness, credibility, and responsibility.

The Power of Investigative Journalism

Investigative journalism involves in-depth research, analysis, and reporting to uncover information not readily available to the public. It aims to expose wrongdoing, corruption, or other issues of public interest that might otherwise remain hidden. Unlike news reporting, which covers current events, and feature writing, which focuses on human interest stories, investigative journalism delves deeper into specific topics or issues.

Confidentiality of sources is crucial in investigative journalism. Protecting sources' identities encourages whistleblowers and insiders to come forward with valuable information. This confidentiality is vital in a democracy, as it helps ensure transparency and accountability in government and other institutions by allowing journalists to uncover misconduct and hold those in power accountable.

However, there are potential drawbacks to source confidentiality. In some cases, it can lead to the disclosure of inaccurate or malicious information, undermining journalists' credibility and causing confusion or social unrest. Journalists must carefully vet sources and corroborate information to minimize the risk of spreading misinformation.

Real-Life Examples

Investigative journalism played a pivotal role in uncovering corruption during the Watergate scandal. Reporters Bob Woodward and Carl Bernstein of The Washington Post investigated the break-in at the Democratic National Committee headquarters, leading to the resignation of President Richard Nixon.

Their reporting exposed a web of corruption within the Nixon administration, demonstrating the power of investigative journalism to hold those in power accountable.

Yet, investigative journalism can also contribute to confusion and unrest when based on faulty information. In 2003, The New York Times published articles claiming Iraq possessed weapons of mass destruction (WMDs), helping build the case for the United States' invasion of Iraq. These claims were later found to be inaccurate, highlighting how investigative journalism, when based on unreliable sources, can inadvertently contribute to misinformation and its consequences.

The Influence of Political Satire

Political satire, characterized by its sharp wit and humor, serves as a critical lens through which to examine and lampoon political leaders, governmental bodies, and prevailing beliefs. By employing techniques such as irony, exaggeration, and parody, this form of entertainment sheds light on societal issues, aiming to provoke reflection and inspire change.

Satire Through Time

Throughout history, the roots of political satire can be traced to ancient Greece, where renowned playwrights like Aristophanes skillfully used satire to lampoon politicians, intellectuals, and established customs. This enduring tradition of using humor as a tool for social commentary showcases the power of satire to challenge the status quo and spark meaningful discourse on pertinent political and social topics.

Political satire served as a means of social control by allowing citizens to openly criticize those in power without fear of reprisal. By satirizing political figures and institutions, playwrights could highlight corruption, incompetence, and hypocrisy, thereby holding leaders accountable and encouraging them to govern responsibly. This helped maintain stability by providing an outlet for dissent and preventing discontent from boiling over into rebellion or unrest.

The Power and Perils of Political Satire

While it can be a potent force for sparking dialogue and challenging the status quo, political satire also grapples with the subjectivity of humor. What one person finds hilarious, another may deem offensive or insensitive. This variability poses a risk: satire can inadvertently trivialize serious issues or perpetuate harmful stereotypes, leading to misunderstandings or unintended consequences. In some cases, satire may struggle to convey complex political ideas or instigate meaningful change, particularly in societies where freedom of speech is restricted or political discourse is polarized.

Ethical considerations loom large in the realm of political satire. While it enjoys protection as a form of free speech in many democratic societies, its impact can reverberate far beyond mere jest. Satirical portrayals of politicians or public figures, while often intended in jest, can stain reputations and erode trust, potentially impairing their ability to govern effectively.

Despite these ethical tightropes, political satire remains an invaluable tool for dissent and accountability in democratic societies. It serves as a check on power, fostering public debate and ensuring that leaders remain answerable to the people they serve. Without satire's ability to lampoon political authority, dissenting voices could be stifled, marginalizing those who dare to question the status quo and eroding the vibrancy of democracy.

In a world where political satire is absent, dissenting individuals might turn to alternative avenues for expressing discontent. Peaceful demonstrations, civil disobedience, and advocacy through traditional media channels could all fill the void left by satire's absence. However, these avenues lack satire's unique ability to engage and mobilize the public through humor. Moreover, without satire's critical lens, there's a risk that leaders could become insulated from scrutiny, eroding the foundation of democratic stability. Thus, the absence of satire could pose a threat to the very system it seeks to critique and uphold.

The Future of Political Communication

In the digital age, characterized by rapid technological advancements, political discourse has undergone a substantial transformation. This shift has been primarily driven by the widespread adoption and accessibility of online platforms, coupled with the emergence of sophisticated artificial intelligence tools. These developments have not only revolutionized the way information is exchanged and opinions are shared but have also created a complex landscape with both advantages and drawbacks. Despite the opportunities for enhanced connectivity and information dissemination, there exist significant challenges, such as the spread of misinformation and the polarization of viewpoints.

Misinformation and Disinformation

One of the paramount challenges faced in the current political sphere is the pervasive proliferation of misinformation and disinformation, which continues to exert a significant influence on public opinion and decision-making processes. The ubiquitous availability of online platforms has empowered individuals from diverse backgrounds to disseminate misleading content, whether by design or by accident. This unrestricted flow of distorted information not only jeopardizes the credibility of public discussions but also erodes the very foundations of democratic governance by sowing seeds of doubt and discord among citizens. In an age where information travels at lightning speed, the imperative to combat the dissemination of falsehoods remains a critical endeavor in safeguarding the integrity of public discourse and upholding the principles of a well-informed and participatory society.

The propagation of misinformation and disinformation in today's digital age can largely be linked to multiple contributing factors, among which echo chambers, algorithmic biases, and the presence of malicious actors play a significant role. Specifically, within the realm of social media platforms, the algorithms used often prioritize the display of content based on levels of user engagement. This approach tends to foster the creation of echo chambers where individuals exist in a digital realm, largely exposed to information that aligns with their preexisting beliefs. Consequently, this perpetuation of confirmation bias not only perpetuates divisions within society but also undermines the potential for meaningful and constructive discourse among differing viewpoints.

These malicious actors capitalize on the inherent lack of centralized control in online platforms, enabling them to manipulate and distort information for nefarious objectives. By exploiting the multifaceted nature of the digital landscape, they are able to propagate deceptive narratives that aim to manipulate public perceptions or create divisions within society. Through the cloak of anonymity and the vast scope of the internet, these actors can significantly magnify the impact of their actions, posing significant threats to the integrity of democratic processes and societal stability.

Fake News

The rampant proliferation of fake news in today's digital era significantly exacerbates the already daunting task of addressing and countering the spread of misinformation and disinformation. This modern issue is further complicated by the fact that, unlike the well-established procedures and rigorous fact-checking protocols observed in traditional journalism, online platforms serve as an ideal environment for the swift production and widespread sharing of deceptive narratives presented with the veneer of authentic news, making it arduous to discern truth from falsehood in this fast-paced information landscape.

The rapid spread and perpetuation of fake news in today's digital age present a significant hurdle for fact-checking initiatives. It becomes increasingly challenging to stem the dissemination of false narratives, even after they have been proven inaccurate. Furthermore, the diminishing confidence in established media sources and the emergence of echo chambers shaped by political affiliations heighten individuals' vulnerability to misinformation. These factors collectively contribute to deepening societal rifts and polarizations, ultimately impeding efforts to promote informed discourse and shared understanding among diverse groups.

Virtual Spaces for Political Participation

The emergence of virtual spaces for political participation has significantly transformed accessibility to the political process by enabling individuals to actively participate in civic discourse and advocacy efforts without leaving the confines of their homes. These online platforms serve as dynamic hubs for fostering dialogue, providing avenues for grassroots activism through petition platforms, and facilitating direct interaction with elected officials through virtual town halls.

However, the effectiveness of virtual spaces for political engagement hinges on establishing and nurturing inclusive and deliberative environments conducive to fostering constructive conversations. The anonymity that online platforms often offer can empower individuals to exhibit unbecoming behavior, such as engaging in harassment, trolling, or spreading hate speech. This unfortunate aspect can detrimentally impact meaningful discourse and, in turn, marginalize certain voices, potentially depleting the richness and diversity of perspectives within the dialogue space. As such, maintaining a balance between fostering open discussions and enforcing codes of conduct to deter harmful behavior is essential for sustaining the integrity and effectiveness of virtual political engagement platforms.

AI in Politics

Artificial intelligence (AI) has significantly transformed the landscape of politics by offering an array of powerful tools for data analysis, predictive modeling, and precise targeted messaging. These AI algorithms possess the capability to sift through extensive datasets, allowing for the identification of intricate patterns, accurate predictions of voter behavior, and the optimization of campaigning strategies with unparalleled accuracy and efficiency. Nevertheless, with the growing reliance on AI within the political sphere, legitimate concerns have arisen regarding algorithmic bias, potential privacy infringements, and the manipulation of public opinion.

The issue of algorithmic bias becomes especially poignant because the impartiality of AI algorithms is fundamentally dependent on the quality and fairness of the data on which they are trained. Biases inherent in the training data can perpetuate and even exacerbate existing social inequalities and disparities. Consequently, a critical examination of the data used to train these algorithms is imperative to mitigate the risk of biases influencing outcomes in ways that perpetuate societal injustices.

The utilization of AI-driven microtargeting techniques in political advertising brings forth ethical considerations surrounding the customization of messaging and the potential ramifications of such precision targeting. By tailoring content to cater to individual preferences and exploiting vulnerabilities, political entities can effectively employ AI algorithms to foster discord, diminish voter engagement, and undermine the sincerity and fairness of the electoral system. The ethical dimensions of utilizing AI in political messaging underline the necessity of stringent scrutiny and accountability in the deployment of these advanced technologies across the political spectrum.

Digital Interaction and Democratic Communication

The advent of digital interaction has altered the landscape of democratic communication, offering new avenues for civic engagement and political participation. Social media platforms serve as virtual town squares where individuals can share ideas, mobilize support, and hold public figures accountable.

However, the nature of digital interaction poses challenges to democratic communication, as online discourse often unfolds amidst a cacophony of competing voices and perspectives. The anonymity and disinhibition afforded by online platforms can foster incivility, echo chambers, and filter bubbles, hindering meaningful dialogue and consensus-building.

Moreover, the algorithmic curation of content on social media platforms can exacerbate polarization and diminish the diversity of viewpoints represented in online discourse. Rather than fostering deliberation and compromise, social media algorithms often prioritize sensationalized content and partisan narratives, reinforcing existing biases and deepening societal divisions.

The contemporary landscape marked by the pervasive spread of misinformation and disinformation, the proliferation of fake news, the emergence of virtual platforms for political engagement, and the growing influence of artificial intelligence in the political sphere serves as a clarion call for heightened vigilance, amplified critical thinking, and increased civic involvement in the digital era. It is imperative to recognize that while the digital realm presents unparalleled opportunities for global interconnectedness and rapid dissemination of information, it also carries significant hazards that can jeopardize the very essence of democratic norms and principles.

To effectively navigate and mitigate these risks, a comprehensive strategy that integrates elements of media literacy instruction, stringent regulatory frameworks, and innovative technological solutions is essential. By prioritizing values such as transparency, accountability, and inclusivity in online interactions and discourse, we can leverage the immense transformative capacities of digital tools to fortify the foundations of democratic governance and cultivate a populace that is not only better informed but also more actively engaged in the democratic process, thereby fortifying the core tenets of our societies.

Chapter 9:

America and the World Stage: Be a Good Neighbor

The United States stands as a central thread, weaving its influence across continents and shaping the course of global events. From economic prowess to military might, the U.S. wields significant power on the world stage, assuming roles ranging from global superpower to diplomatic mediator.

Yet, amidst its prominence, challenges loom large, from navigating complex geopolitical dynamics to addressing important issues like climate change and international security threats.

American Politics' Global Impact

Today, countries understand the importance of working together through groups like the United Nations (UN) and North Atlantic Treaty Organization (NATO) to keep peace. These groups help countries talk, solve problems, and stay safe from things like wars, terrorism, and climate issues.

They show that problems affecting everyone need everyone's help to fix them.

Key Milestones: The United States' Impact on Global History

Throughout history, the United States has played significant roles that shaped the global landscape:

- **The American Revolution (1775–1783)** marked the nation's birth, breaking free from British rule and establishing democratic governance.

- In **World War I (1917–1918)**, the US sided with the Allies, tipping the balance and contributing to victory.

- **The Great Depression (1929–1939)** brought economic turmoil globally. President Roosevelt's New Deal policies helped stabilize the economy.

- During **World War II (1941–1945)**, the US entered after the attack on Pearl Harbor, pivotal in defeating the Axis powers and shaping the post-war order.

- **The Yalta Conference (1945)** laid foundations for international institutions like the UN, shaping the Cold War era.

From Cold War to Superpower

During the Cold War, the world was split into two blocs: the Western Bloc, led by the US and defined by capitalist democracy, and the Eastern Bloc, led by the Soviet Union with communist ideology.

The US took the helm of the Western Bloc, working to curb communism's spread and champion democratic values globally. Initiatives like the Marshall Plan aided post-war Europe's reconstruction and countered communism's advance.

This era saw intense rivalry and conflict, from proxy wars to nuclear threats. The US utilized military alliances like NATO and intervened in conflicts like the Korean and Vietnam Wars to counter Soviet influence.

The Cold War concluded with the Soviet Union's collapse in 1991, marking the US' triumph and the victory of capitalism and democracy. The Berlin Wall's fall signaled Germany's reunification and the end of Europe's division.

As the sole superpower, the US held unmatched influence in military, economic, and cultural spheres. Its democratic ideals and free market capitalism shaped the post-Cold War world.

American Influence in a Post-Cold War World

In the post-Cold War era, the United States solidified its status as the primary nexus of influence, asserting its impact through a combination of economic supremacy, cutting-edge technological advancements, and robust military prowess. Its pervasive soft power was further bolstered as American culture, language, and values permeated various facets of global media, entertainment, and consumer landscapes.

While championing fundamental ideals like democracy, human rights, and respect for national autonomy, the United States, as the leading global superpower, ignited contentious discussions and disputes. Detractors raised concerns over instances of American unilateral approaches, interventionist strategies, and perceived breaches of international legal norms—notably evident in military campaigns undertaken in regions such as Iraq and Afghanistan.

Challenges and Benefits of American Hegemony

The United States' role as the primary center of power on the global stage brought about a myriad of possibilities and complexities for other nations. Aligning closely with the United States offered a spectrum of advantages, ranging from the security assurances it provided to the numerous economic boons, along with the valuable access to worldwide markets and cutting-edge technology. However, this alliance also introduced a conundrum, given the potential hazards associated with dependence, erosion of self-governance, and the perils of being drawn into geopolitical conflicts.

The United States' active military interventions in regions considered to pose threats to the established global order stirred widespread apprehension regarding the deployment of force without the necessary international consensus or authorization. Against the backdrop of evolving transnational challenges such as terrorism and the proliferation of weapons of mass destruction, the ongoing discussions surrounding the delicate equilibrium between individual national sovereignty and the imperative for unified collective security have grown notably more poignant and unresolved.

Global Progress and Challenges

During the post-Cold War period, the international community saw a notable shift towards embracing democratic values, human rights, and sovereignty respect despite encountering various challenges. This movement towards shared ideals was facilitated by multilateral organizations, with the United Nations playing a pivotal role in fostering dialogue, cooperation, and conflict resolution, although its effectiveness was sometimes constrained by limitations and imperfections.

Additionally, the global landscape witnessed a significant transition characterized by the spread of democratic governance and the waning influence of authoritarian regimes, leading to a greater emphasis on political pluralism and civic engagement worldwide. Nevertheless, the persistence of social inequalities, injustices, and conflicts underscored the continuous struggle to fully realize the principles of peace, equality, and justice on a worldwide scale.

The United States emerged as a central player in shaping the contemporary world order, with its historical commitment to democratic principles and independence, its influential role in the Cold War era, and its status as a primary global power post-Cold War. While American dominance has brought about both advantages and complications for the international community, the pursuit of a planet characterized by peace, justice, and equality continues to be a common goal shared by nations across the globe.

The Influence of American Politics on Global Governance

The United States' influence on global governance has been profound and multifaceted, shaping the course of international affairs in significant ways throughout history. From President Wilson's visionary principles during the aftermath of World War I to pivotal moments like the end of World War II, Kennedy's visit to Berlin, the Cuban Missile Crisis, and the fight against the spread of Communism, American politics has consistently played a central role in shaping the global order.

Wilson's 14 Points and the Peace of Versailles

In 1917, the United States entered the war on the side of the Allied Powers against the Central Powers. When the balance tilted in favor of the Allies, US President Woodrow Wilson took the initiative to formulate "conditions for peace" with 14 points, on January 8, 1918.

The points included a "utopian" vision of the world after World War I; outlined a policy of free trade, open agreements; and democracy; emphasized the need for national self-determination for various ethnic groups in Europe; and called for a negotiated end to the war; international disarmament; and the withdrawal of the Central Powers from occupied territories.

Wilson also proposed the establishment of a general league whose mission would be to mediate international disputes to prevent any future wars, and this association later became known as the "League of Nations."

However, the main allies of the United States of America found these points too idealistic and unworkable. As for the Germans, they believed that Wilson's vision would form the cornerstone of any future peace treaty, but the "Treaty of Versailles" later proved that they were completely wrong.

Even after the terms of peace and Wilson's 14 points were defined, the curtain did not fall (on the part of international law) on the conflicts of World War I until after lengthy negotiations at the Paris Peace Conference, which resulted in the signing of 5 treaties with the defeated countries, including the Treaty of Versailles with Germany, and the Treaty of San Germain with Austria, the Treaty of Nobi with Bulgaria, the Treaty of Trianon with Hungary, and the Treaty of Sèvres with the Ottoman Empire.

Global borders were redrawn based on the Treaty of Versailles and the subsequent treaties that imposed their terms on the defeated countries that were not parties to the negotiations. New borders were drawn for some countries and countries that had not existed before were created. Therefore, the properties of the Ottoman Empire and Germany's colonies outside Europe were divided. Germany divided itself.

Rise of American Hegemony

Immediately after World War II, all the countries of Europe and Asia emerged economically and militarily exhausted, unlike the United States of America, which developed into the first power in the world. The United Nations was established in April 1945. The Bretton Woods Agreements, which created the Bank The goal of the Global Monetary Fund and the International Monetary Fund, was to restructure the economies of developed countries and to benefit from the mistakes committed after World War I, which led to the collapse of the monetary and financial system immediately after the 1929 crisis.

Following the devastation of World War II, world leaders sought to create an organization that would prevent future conflicts and foster a cooperative international environment. Key objectives included maintaining global peace through collective security, advancing human rights, and promoting social and economic development.   The UN aimed to provide a platform for dialogue among nations, enabling the peaceful resolution of disputes and the establishment of norms governing international behavior. Additionally, it sought to address humanitarian issues, such as poverty, hunger, and health crises, while fostering sustainable development and protecting the environment. Another significant goal was to uphold international law and support decolonization efforts, ensuring that all people had the right to self-determination. Through these initiatives, the UN aspired to create a more just, stable, and prosperous world.

One of the important consequences of World War II was that America had become a first-world power and needed a market to export its products. Therefore, it carried out the reconstruction of Europe (the Marshall Plan), so American hegemony continued until the 1960s, when a set of problems appeared to confront it. The first is that Europe and Japan have become competing powers for the United States of America due to the improvement in the standard of living of their citizens. The second of these problems is that a group of countries have become dissatisfied with this reality imposed on them as a result of the Yalta Agreement (Vietnam, Algeria, and Cuba).

China, for its part, also refused to comply with the directives of the Soviet Union, which suggested that it sign a peace agreement with the National Party of Taiwan, which demands independence from China, the motherland.

Starting in 1970s , Europe and Japan became partners after being affiliated with the United States of America. For this reason, the World Economic Forum was established in Davos in 1971 and the Group of Seven Countries (G7) in 1976. Since this period, the American administration, led by President Nixon, sensed that American leadership was in danger, so he issued his historic decision to make the U.S. dollar the internationally accepted currency instead of gold.

Key Cold War Moments: Kennedy in Berlin and the Cuban Missile Crisis

During the Cold War, American politics wielded a significant impact on global governance by engaging in confrontations with the Soviet

Union and actively working to curb the spread of communism. Through President John F. Kennedy's historic visit to Berlin in 1963, the United States solidified its unyielding dedication to upholding freedom and democracy amidst Soviet hostility. His iconic declaration, "Ich bin ein Berliner," not only resonated deeply with the citizens of Berlin but also served as a powerful reaffirmation of America's solidarity with its allies in the relentless fight against the oppressive grasp of Communist rule.

Additionally, the Cuban Missile Crisis of 1962 emerged as a pivotal juncture in international governance, heralding a perilous moment where the world teetered on the edge of a potentially catastrophic nuclear conflict. Kennedy's adept diplomatic maneuvering and resolute stance when facing off against Soviet Premier Nikita Khrushchev's decision to station nuclear missiles in Cuba ultimately averted a disaster of unparalleled proportions, shining a spotlight on the critical importance of adept crisis management and open dialogue in the realm of global relations. This crisis vividly underscored the pressing necessity for robust arms control frameworks and disarmament measures to effectively stave off the dangerous escalation of tensions between nuclear superpowers and to promote lasting peace and stability on the global stage.

Cold War Legacy and Modern Geopolitics

Throughout the Cold War, American politics was characterized by its unwavering commitment to containing the spread of communism, defending democracy, and advancing free-market capitalism worldwide. From the Korean War, where the US fought to halt Communist aggression, to the protracted conflict in Vietnam, where American forces battled the Viet Cong and North Vietnamese, the United States intervened militarily in various regions to thwart Communist expansionism and safeguard its strategic interests. These interventions, although a subject of intense debate and criticism, underscored America's far-reaching geopolitical objectives and its position as a dominant global power that championed ideological principles.

The dissolution of the Soviet Union in 1991 altered the global landscape, bringing the Cold War era to a close and reshaping the dynamics of international governance. With the disappearance of its primary Cold War foe, the United States ascended as the preeminent superpower, wielding unprecedented influence in shaping worldwide events and policies. Nevertheless, the enduring effects of the Cold War persist in contemporary geopolitics, exemplified by the enduring tensions between the United States and Russia, as well as the rekindling of major power rivalries, especially in regions like Eastern Europe and the Asia-Pacific, where geopolitical maneuvering and strategic competition continue to shape the world order.

The Influence of American Foreign Policy on Global Trade

Capitalism is an economic system where businesses are privately owned, aiming to make profits through market competition. Global trade is crucial in capitalism, allowing countries to trade goods, services, and money worldwide.

The United States is a big player in global trade, both importing and exporting various goods, technology, and financial resources. It became an economic powerhouse due to factors like natural resources, innovation, and favorable policies. The US trades with many nations, forming alliances that boost growth but also facing challenges like trade imbalances.

After the Cold War, the US emerged as a dominant global power, while Europe formed the EU and adopted the euro to rival the US dollar. However, new economic giants like China have emerged, challenging U.S. dominance. To stay competitive, the US focuses on innovation and trade deals.

The US has allies like Canada and Mexico, but also competitors like China. It leads in technology, finance, and entertainment but faces issues like income inequality and infrastructure problems. From its inception, the United States relied heavily on the transfer of technology from Great Britain to modernize industry. This reliance prompted

Alexander Hamilton, one of the Founding Fathers of the United States, to write his Report on Manufacturers in 1791, in which he called for support of emerging industries that provided "the essentials of the national supply," including "the means of subsistence, habitation, clothing, and defense." Hamilton supported the limited use of "grants" as "a kind of direct and positive encouragement." He proposed supporting only a limited number of new industries, such as coal, raw wool, sailcloth, cotton, and glass.

The United States supported international rules in response to the rise of subsidy policy in the 1960s and 1970s. For example, during the negotiation of the Subsidies and Countervailing Measures (SCM) Agreement, the United States lobbied for its successful adoption to reach acceptable provisions for adjusting subsidies or countervailing duties based on US law and practice.

Currently, there is an American consensus between the Democratic and Republican parties regarding the inadequacy of existing institutions to deal with global crises, such as epidemics, climate change, and the rise of China. The previous administration of President Donald Trump adopted the "America First" policy, which included policies such as prioritizing domestic production of "Covid-19" vaccines or imposing tariffs on billions of dollars in Chinese imports. With the change in the US administration, the Biden administration maintained the Trump administration's tariff policy, and expanded its scope to help the United States compete globally against a rising China. The goals of current efforts are divided into confronting China and combating climate change.

The Role of the American Government on World Affairs

The United States holds a crucial role in global affairs, engaging in various international organizations and taking stances on critical issues such as nuclear disarmament, environmental challenges, military intervention, immigration policies, international funding, and democracy promotion.

Nuclear Disarmament

The US has been a significant player in nuclear disarmament efforts, participating in negotiations within the UN and other forums to promote non-proliferation and disarmament initiatives. Its stance on specific treaties and agreements may vary depending on the administration in power and geopolitical considerations.

Treaty of Paris and Environmental Challenges

The US played a crucial role in negotiating the Paris Agreement under the Obama administration, aimed at combating climate change. However, it withdrew from the agreement under President Trump and rejoined it under the Biden administration, signaling a renewed commitment to addressing environmental challenges globally.

Military Intervention

The US has a history of military intervention justified on grounds of national security, humanitarian intervention, or democracy promotion. Its military involvement ranges from direct interventions to supporting international peacekeeping missions authorized by the UN Security Council. However, these interventions are often debated for their legality, effectiveness, and long-term consequences.

Immigration Policies

The US has a complex relationship with immigration, influencing its engagement with international organizations such as the United Nations High Commissioner for Refugees (UNHCR) and the International Organization for Migration (IOM). While traditionally a major contributor to global refugee resettlement efforts, U.S.

immigration policies have been subject to change and sometimes restrictive measures, particularly under certain administrations.

International Funding

As a major economic power, the United States provides significant financial support to various international organizations and initiatives, including humanitarian aid, development assistance, peacekeeping operations, and global health programs. However, funding levels and burden-sharing among member states can vary due to political debates and budget constraints.

Strategies for Defending Democracy and Promoting Progress

The US employs diplomatic engagement, economic assistance, technical support, military intervention—in some cases—and cultural diplomacy to defend democracy and promote progress in other countries. These strategies aim to advocate for democratic principles, support democratic transitions, strengthen democratic institutions, and promote American values of freedom and human rights.

- **Diplomatic Engagement:** The US uses its diplomatic influence to advocate for democratic principles and human rights in bilateral and multilateral forums, supporting democratic transitions and condemning human rights abuses.

- **Economic Assistance:** Economic aid supports democratic governance, civil society development, and economic reforms in countries transitioning to democracy or recovering from conflict, aiming to promote political stability and economic prosperity.

- **Technical Support:** The US provides technical assistance and capacity-building programs to strengthen democratic institutions, promote free and fair elections, and foster civic engagement, helping defend against threats to democracy.

- **Military Intervention:** Although controversial, the US has intervened militarily to support democratic movements or overthrow authoritarian regimes deemed threats to regional stability or US interests, though these interventions can have unintended consequences.

- **Cultural Diplomacy:** Through exchange programs, educational initiatives, media outreach, and public diplomacy efforts, the US promotes democratic values and ideals abroad, emphasizing freedom, democracy, and human rights.

The US plays a significant role in shaping global affairs through its participation in international organizations, advocacy for democracy and human rights, and engagement with other nations to address shared challenges and promote progress. However, its approach is subject to evolving priorities, domestic politics, and leadership changes, impacting its effectiveness and consistency in pursuing foreign policy objectives.

Chapter 10:

Voices of Change and Resilience

Political participation is the heartbeat of democracy, empowering people to shape their communities and work toward the common good. There are many ways individuals can get involved, from grassroots activism to institutional engagement. By delving into how participation drives social change and promotes unity, we uncover its vital role in creating a fairer, more inclusive society.

In today's world, where challenges like inequality and injustice loom large, political participation is more important than ever. Through collective action and civic engagement, we can protect democracy, uphold human rights, and build a better future for everyone.

Activism Through Art and Culture

Art and culture have long served as powerful tools for social and political activism, offering avenues for expression, identity formation, political critique, education, and fostering social integration. Scholars and real-life examples vividly illustrate how art and culture can catalyze change and address societal issues.

- **Expression and Identity:** Art allows individuals and communities to share their stories and assert their identities. For example, during the Harlem Renaissance, African American artists celebrated their culture and challenged racial stereotypes through literature and music.

- **Political Critique:** Artists use their platforms to challenge injustice and question the status quo. Banksy's street art, like "Girl with Balloon," prompts viewers to reflect on societal issues such as war and consumerism.

- **Education:** Art serves as a tool for educating and raising awareness. Ava DuVernay's documentary "13th" exposes systemic racism in the criminal justice system, encouraging viewers to confront uncomfortable truths.

- **Social Integration:** Cultural events like Burning Man foster community and connection through participatory art and collaboration, creating inclusive spaces where people can express themselves freely.

- **Well-being:** Engaging with art and culture promotes well-being by fostering empathy, understanding, and a sense of belonging.

Examples

The Woodstock music festival of 1969 exemplified the countercultural spirit of the era, promoting peace, love, and anti-establishment values. Its impact extended far beyond music, contributing to the anti-war movement and advocating for civil rights.

Similarly, the MeToo movement gained momentum with the support of influential figures in Hollywood who spoke out against sexual harassment and assault. The courage of these individuals, along with the power of social media to amplify their voices, led to a global reckoning with issues of gender inequality and abuse of power in various industries.

Both movements demonstrate the transformative potential of art and culture in inspiring social and political change, rallying people around shared values, and challenging entrenched power structures.

The Legacy of Civil Rights Movements

The Civil Rights Movement in the United States was a crucial fight for equality, primarily focusing on the rights of African Americans but also paving the way for progress in other marginalized communities. It emerged in the mid-20th century in response to widespread racial segregation, discrimination, and violence, particularly in the Southern states. After the Civil War, African Americans gained citizenship and voting rights, but these were eroded by Jim Crow laws enforcing segregation. The movement gained traction in the 1950s and 1960s, triggered by events like the Brown v. Board of Education ruling against school segregation and Rosa Parks' refusal to give up her bus seat, leading to the Montgomery Bus Boycott.

Key Figures

- **Rosa Parks:** Her defiance sparked the Montgomery Bus Boycott and energized the movement.

- **Martin Luther King Jr.:** Known for advocating nonviolent resistance, King's leadership was central, notably in the March on Washington and his "I Have a Dream" speech.

- **Malcolm X:** Initially promoting Black separatism, Malcolm X later embraced a more inclusive approach to civil rights.

- **Thurgood Marshall:** A pioneering attorney who argued successfully in the Brown case and became the first African American Supreme Court justice.

Achievements

The movement achieved significant victories, including the Civil Rights Act of 1964, which outlawed discrimination, and the Voting Rights Act of 1965, aimed at removing barriers to voting.

Ongoing Challenges

The movement's legacy is profound, inspiring progress in civil liberties and sparking movements for women's rights, LGBTQIA+ rights, and environmental justice. However, challenges persist:

- **Women's Rights:** Issues like pay equity and reproductive rights remain.

- **LGBTQIA+ Rights:** Discrimination in employment, housing, and healthcare persists.

- **Legalization of Abortion:** Debates over abortion access and reproductive healthcare continue.

- **Environmental Rights:** Communities of color bear the brunt of environmental degradation.

- **Ethnic Discrimination:** Racial and ethnic minorities face systemic biases in education, healthcare, and the justice system.

Government and Political Responses

Governments and political parties have enacted legislation, but progress faces resistance. Activist groups, cultural and scientific figures, and grassroots movements play vital roles in pushing for change.

Though progress has been made, barriers like legislative rollbacks, voter suppression, and cultural biases persist. However, the determination of activists and marginalized communities fuels momentum for change, highlighting the ongoing struggle for civil rights in the US.

Immigrant Narratives and Political Advocacy

The issue of immigration in the United States encompasses an array of challenges, including legal settlement, housing availability, access to healthcare and education, labor market dynamics, and integration into society. Whether this should be considered a problem depends on different viewpoints, but it's evident that immigration carries significant socio-economic and political implications.

Legal Settlement

Immigration laws and policies regulate who can legally settle in the country. Concerns often arise regarding the influx of undocumented immigrants and the potential strain on resources and infrastructure. However, it's important to recognize the valuable contributions immigrants make to the economy and society, both through their labor and cultural diversity.

Accommodation and Housing Facilities

The growing immigrant population increases demand for housing, potentially leading to competition and increased costs, especially in urban areas. Moreover, inadequate housing conditions can result from overcrowding or exploitation by landlords, posing challenges to immigrant communities.

Access to Health and Education

Immigrants, particularly those without legal status, may encounter obstacles in accessing healthcare and education due to legal barriers or language differences. This can result in disparities in health outcomes and educational opportunities, impacting individual well-being and overall societal welfare.

Labor Market

Immigrants play vital roles in various sectors of the economy, yet concerns about job competition and wage suppression for native workers persist. Additionally, undocumented immigrants are vulnerable to exploitation and abuse in the workplace because of their legal status, posing challenges to labor market fairness.

Integration/Discrimination

Successful integration into society is often hindered by discrimination and xenophobia, which can impede immigrants' social and economic participation. Conversely, promoting integration benefits both immigrants and the wider community by fostering social cohesion and economic prosperity.

Political Campaigns and Proposals

Immigration has been a focal point in political campaigns, with candidates proposing diverse approaches, from strict enforcement to comprehensive reform. Over time, the discourse has shifted, reflecting changing attitudes and priorities, with recent emphasis on pathways to citizenship, visa program reform, and addressing root causes of migration.

Civil Discourse Changes

Public discussions on immigration have evolved amidst shifting demographics, economic conditions, and political rhetoric. While debates remain polarized, recent years have seen increased inclusivity and recognition of immigrants' humanity, driven by grassroots movements challenging stereotypes and advocating for immigrant rights.

Resilience in the Face of Adversity

Resilience, an extensively utilized term within various fields including but not limited to psychology, environmental science, and engineering, serves as an increasingly pertinent concept in the realms of politics and society. In essence, resilience represents the intrinsic capacity possessed by individuals, communities, and entire societies to not only withstand but also adapt to and ultimately recover from diverse forms of adversity and challenges. When considering this concept within the sphere of political dynamics, resilience takes on a distinctive meaning denoting the intrinsic ability of a political system as a whole, encompassing its institutions, governance structures, and citizenry, to not only endure but also effectively rebound from unforeseen crises and disruptions, be they economic recessions, social upheavals, or natural calamities. This critical resilience attribute enables political systems to remain stable, responsive, and capable of navigating turbulent waters with steadfast resolve and adaptability.

Resilience in Political and Social Crises

Historical events such as the September 11 attacks and the COVID-19 pandemic offer poignant illustrations of the critical nature of societal resilience. In the aftermath of 9/11, the United States grappled not only with a profound loss of life but also with a dire threat to its national security and social fabric. The resilience exhibited by the American people following the tragedy, marked by a unifying spirit and a surge of patriotism, served as a powerful testament to the cohesive strength of society in the face of terror.

Likewise, the global landscape was severely tested by the impact of the COVID-19 pandemic, challenging resilience across various fronts including health, economy, and social structures. Countries that displayed exceptional resilience were those that effectively controlled the spread of the virus while simultaneously providing robust economic support to their citizens, and fostering social unity despite the upheavals caused by significant lifestyle adjustments and restrictions.

Building a Resilient Society

To enhance resilience and effectively manage adversity, societies need to adopt collaborative and constructive actions. These actions include strengthening democratic institutions to ensure transparent, accountable governance and protecting civil liberties, thus reducing conflict likelihood. Encouraging community engagement and active participation in communal activities enhances social bonds and support, which is essential during crises. Investing in education and communication is crucial, as well-informed citizens are better equipped to make decisions that promote resilience. This includes focusing on emotional intelligence and conflict resolution, in addition to traditional skills and knowledge.

Economic resilience can be built by developing diverse and adaptable economies less vulnerable to shocks, supporting small businesses, promoting innovation, and protecting workers. Enhancing both physical and technological infrastructures ensures that services can continue uninterrupted during crises and aids in rapid recovery.

Empowering Citizen Participation for Future Resilience

Citizen participation plays a crucial role in building societal resilience. Engaged citizens contribute to a vibrant civil society, engage in political processes, and volunteer during crises, thus enhancing overall community resilience. Educational systems that emphasize civic responsibility and platforms that promote dialogue between citizens and government can further bolster this participation.

Looking forward, societies face challenges such as climate change, technological disruptions, geopolitical tensions, and demographic shifts that could test their resilience. Societies can prepare by developing adaptive policies, fostering inclusivity to ensure all society segments are involved in resilience-building efforts, leveraging technology to improve emergency responses and facilitate community engagement, and promoting global cooperation to tackle challenges no single nation can manage alone.

Resilience is a multifaceted concept that encapsulates not only the ability to rebound from setbacks but also the capacity to grow and transform in the face of difficulties. This process of resilience is nourished by proactive measures, such as thorough preparation, active involvement from all perspectives, and a willingness to adapt to changing circumstances. Looking ahead, as communities navigate the certain challenges that lie ahead, the cultivation of a resilient mindset becomes pivotal in lessening the negative repercussions, fostering harmony, diminishing sources of discord, and ultimately preserving a vibrant, harmonious, and secure communal existence.

Chapter 11:

The American Dream: Vote in Your Own Best Interest

The act of voting is not just a personal choice but a powerful way to influence society and our collective future. When we vote, we do more than fulfill a duty; we express our hopes and values and shape the world around us. Consider how your single vote can impact policies and affect the lives of many. Let's see how each vote helps to drive change and maintain continuity in our society.

Young Voters' Perspectives

Young or first-time voters often hesitate to participate in elections due to doubts about the impact of their vote, a lack of information about the candidates or issues, or disillusionment with the political process. Many feel disconnected, thinking their single vote can't change the outcome, or they distrust the political system.

Despite these challenges, engaging young voters is crucial, and real-life experiences can help. Historically, voter turnout among young people has been lower than among older adults. In the 2020 Presidential election, about 46% of eligible voters aged 18 to 29 voted, compared to 68% of those aged 65 and older. However, this represents an increase in youth participation over previous years, driven by higher political engagement on issues like climate change, racial justice, and economic policies. (Pewre Search, 2023).

To increase young voter turnout, it's essential to improve access to voter registration and offer more civic education. Schools and community groups can help by providing non-partisan information on voting procedures and the issues at stake.

Local and state elections, where the results can hinge on just a few votes, demonstrate the significant impact young voters can have. By understanding the direct effects of governmental policies on areas such as education, jobs, and healthcare, young people can see the tangible benefits of their involvement.

First Time Voting

Voting for the first time is a significant milestone that denotes a pivotal shift from mere onlooker to engaged contributor within the democratic landscape. Acquiring a comprehensive grasp of the electoral process and equipping oneself adequately for it not only guarantees the amplification of one's voice but also fortifies the foundation for actively influencing the trajectory of both the local community and the nation at large. By embracing this fundamental right and engaging in the democratic exercise responsibly, individuals can effectively partake in the collective endeavor of shaping the future, playing a vital role in the ongoing narrative of progress and change.

What is Needed?

First and foremost, in order to exercise their right to vote and actively participate in the democratic process, individuals must ensure they are properly registered. Registration deadlines vary depending on the state, highlighting the importance of staying informed and meeting the necessary requirements well in advance. It is worth noting that many states now provide the convenience of online registration, allowing eligible voters to easily navigate the process from their own homes. In addition to online registration, traditional paper registration forms can also be obtained from a variety of locations, including government offices, public libraries, and local community organizations.

Once you have completed the registration process, it is crucial to thoroughly acquaint yourself with the upcoming ballot and the individuals or topics seeking election. This involves delving into the candidates' perspectives, examining their positions on different matters, and grasping the implications of any ballot propositions or measures. A plethora of resources can be accessed on the internet, such as candidate webpages, impartial voter handbooks, and verified governmental websites, which are designed to aid voters in making knowledgeable choices for the upcoming election cycle. Engaging with these resources will empower you to make well-informed decisions when casting your vote.

Election Day

On Election Day or during early voting periods, voters need to visit their designated polling place to exercise their democratic right to vote. This crucial civic duty ensures that their voices are heard in the decision-making process of selecting representatives. The importance of knowing where to cast their ballot cannot be overstated, as it contributes to the integrity and transparency of the electoral process. Obtaining this information is made convenient either through voter registration procedures or by accessing state and local election websites, which provide up-to-date details. It is advisable for voters to come prepared with a valid form of identification, such as a driver's license or passport, as certain states may mandate identity verification prior to voting. This simple step helps safeguard against voter fraud and protects the integrity of the electoral system.

At the polling location, voters approach the election officials stationed at check-in counters, where their registration details undergo thorough verification. This step ensures that the voter is directed to the appropriate booth and provided with clear instructions on how to successfully cast their ballot. Depending on the specific state regulations, voters might encounter the modern electronic voting machines or continue the traditional method of marking paper ballots. Adhering diligently to the given guidelines, regardless of the voting method utilized, is imperative as it guarantees the accurate tabulation of each individual's vote, thereby upholding the integrity of the voting process.

For individuals who opt to cast their vote through the mail-in ballot system, it is imperative to adhere to the prescribed timeline for requesting the ballot and submitting it before the specified cutoff date. Properly following the detailed guidelines accompanying the ballot, which entail correctly completing all fields, affixing signatures where necessary, and promptly dispatching the ballot, guarantees that your vote will be duly accounted for and included in the final tally of votes.

Political Awakening

It's crucial to pause and reflect on our understanding of political affairs and the sources shaping our opinions. Are we actively seeking diverse perspectives, or are we passively absorbing content that reinforces our existing beliefs? Challenge yourself to venture beyond echo chambers, exploring reputable sources with varying viewpoints. By broadening your knowledge base, you not only enrich your understanding but also cultivate a more nuanced perspective on complex issues.

Action is essential for meaningful change. Start by identifying your needs and interests within your community. What issues resonate with you deeply? Whether it's environmental sustainability, social justice, or economic equality, pinpointing your passions is the first step toward impactful advocacy.

Once you've identified your priorities, consider the power of collective action. Reflect on your social circles—the groups you belong to and the individuals you share your life with. How can you leverage these connections to effect positive change? Engage in open dialogue, fostering constructive conversations that inspire empathy and understanding. By collaborating with like-minded peers, you amplify your voices and magnify your impact.

Meaningful change extends beyond individual actions; it requires a fundamental shift in our collective consciousness. Embrace the idea that everyone plays a role within our communities, regardless of background or circumstance. Each voice carries weight, each contribution adds value. By recognizing our interconnectedness, we cultivate a sense of shared responsibility for the well-being of society as a whole.

Consider the long-term implications of your engagement. Sustainable progress requires sustained effort, a commitment to continual learning and adaptation. As you embark on this journey, envision the future you aspire to create. What legacy do you hope to leave for future generations? By investing in political participation today, you lay the groundwork for a more equitable and inclusive tomorrow.

The path to political awakening is not always linear. There will be obstacles, setbacks, and moments of doubt. Yet, in these moments, remember the power of resilience—the ability to persevere in the face of adversity. View challenges as opportunities for growth, learning, and renewal. Your journey is not defined by the obstacles you encounter, but by the courage and conviction with which you navigate them.

Question the status quo, challenge entrenched norms, and advocate for positive change. Your voice matters, your actions have consequences, and your choices shape the world around you.

Political Journey: A Personal Reflection

As individuals traverse the intricate pathways of our political landscape, taking time to pause and reflect on the journey becomes increasingly essential. Observing one's routines, identifying main concerns, and evaluating the actions taken to enact change within one's immediate surroundings are all vital steps in fostering a more engaged and thoughtful citizenship. It is crucial to ask oneself whether active participation in the issues that resonate most deeply is being prioritized or if a passive stance as mere observers of societal narratives is inadvertently adopted.

The power of community and collective action cannot be overstated in this context. Searching for new avenues and groups where voices can be shared and activism can be conducted is an enriching way to deepen involvement in political advocacy. Joining grassroots movements, offering time and effort to local initiatives, and partaking in community forums are but a few examples of the myriad opportunities available to individuals seeking to contribute positively to societal progress.

Although politics has often been perceived as a domain exclusive to a select few, truthfully, it is a transformative tool open to all members of society. Its reach extends far beyond the traditional corridors of power to impact every facet of our daily lives. Recognizing the inherently political nature of interactions and decisions not only gives individuals agency over their own destinies but also empowers them to actively shape the world around them.

Within the cacophony of varying interests and ideologies, the importance of engaging in personal ethical reflection cannot be understated. Defining one's life purpose and selecting the means to accomplish set goals are fundamental aspects of aligning actions with core values.

Political participation plays a dual role—it serves as a vehicle for enacting tangible change while concurrently acting as a mechanism for personal empowerment. In a society often characterized by conflict and discord, engagement in the political sphere provides a means to reclaim agency amidst chaos. Through active involvement in critical issues, individuals transcend the passivity of observation to become agents of change shaping our collective future.

In essence, the individual political journey is deeply personal, intertwining with the human experience. Navigating the labyrinthine corridors of power and influence should not detract from recognizing the inherent power residing within each person. Embracing active roles as political participants empowers individuals to effect positive changes within themselves and the communities they inhabit, fostering a culture of engaged citizenship and impactful advocacy.

Conclusion

Understanding what you're voting for and why is key. It's more than just names on a ballot; it's about grasping the ideas, policies, and visions that candidates and parties stand for. This means doing your homework: researching political platforms, proposals, and where candidates get their campaign funds. Remember, voting isn't a one-time deal—it's an ongoing commitment, with each election shaping our society. Your vote isn't just a number; it's a reflection of your beliefs, values, and hopes for the future.

Making informed decisions is crucial. Novice voters must consider various factors, like a candidate's integrity, competence, and how well their ideas align with personal beliefs. Also, voting isn't the only way to participate; getting involved in campaigns amplifies your voice and lets you shape the conversation.

Beyond the mechanics of elections lies a deeper reflection on civil rights and the power of politics to bring about change. Political engagement isn't just about voting; it's about standing up against oppression, building communities, and working together for the greater good. Every action, big or small, contributes to shaping our society.

Let's not forget the significance of one vote. It's a symbol of your voice, your agency, and your responsibility as a citizen. Each vote matters, and collectively, they shape our nation's direction.

As we wrap up, remember that you have the power to shape the future. By staying informed, participating actively, and standing up for what you believe in, you're not just a spectator—you're a force for change. So, as you navigate the world of politics, never underestimate the impact of your vote, your voice, and your actions. They have the potential to shape our society for the better, now and for generations to come.

References

About - Gender Studies. (n.d.). UCLA. https://gender.ucla.edu/about/

Adler, F. H. (1993). Norberto Bobbio on Liberalism, Socialism and Democracy. *The Polish Sociological Bulletin, 101*, 21–40. http://www.jstor.org/stable/45275260

Arackal, F. (n.d.). *Ethical dimensions of investigative reporting.* Academia.edu. https://www.academia.edu/36357055/Ethical_Dimensions_of_Investigative_Reporting

Blakemore, E. (2018, March 23). *Youth in revolt: Five powerful movements fueled by young activists.* National Geographic. https://www.nationalgeographic.com/culture/article/youth-activism-young-protesters-historic-movements

Clifton, J. (2023, March 1). *Many differences between liberals and conservatives may boil down to one belief.* Scientific American. https://www.scientificamerican.com/article/many-differences-between-liberals-and-conservatives-may-boil-down-to-one-belief/

Democrat vs. republican. (n.d.). Diffen. https://www.diffen.com/difference/Democrat_vs_Republican

Desai, S. & Oehrli, J. A. (2024, March 14). *"Fake news," lies, and propaganda: How to sort facts from fiction.* University of Michigan Library. https://guides.lib.umich.edu/fakenews

Duverger, M. (2024, May 23). *Political party.* Encyclopedia Britannica. https://www.britannica.com/topic/political-party

Ehrenberg, V. (1950). Origins of democracy. *Historia: Zeitschrift Für Alte Geschichte, 1*(4), 515–548. http://www.jstor.org/stable/4434319

Founding fathers quotes on government, democracy, and placing power in the people. (n.d.). Ammo.com. https://ammo.com/articles/founding-fathers-quotes-democracy-government-power-in-people

Froomkin, D. Shapiro, I.& Dahl, R. A. (2024, May 6). *Democracy.* Encyclopedia Britannica. https://www.britannica.com/topic/democracy

Guide to working on political campaigns. (n.d.). Harvard Law School. https://hls.harvard.edu/bernard-koteen-office-of-public-interest-advising/a-quick-guide-to-working-on-political-campaigns/

Halpin, J. & Cook, M. (2010, April 14). *Social movements and progressivism.* Center for American Progress. https://www.americanprogress.org/article/social-movements-and-progressivism/

Killian, L. M., Smelser, N. J., & Turner, R. H. (2024, May 6). *Social movement.* Encyclopedia Britannica. https://www.britannica.com/topic/social-movement

Liberalism, conservatism, and the intellectuals. (n.d.). Princeton University. https://www.princeton.edu/~starr/libcon.html

List of political parties in the United States. (n.d.). Ballotpedia. https://ballotpedia.org/List_of_political_parties_in_the_United_States

Mapping american social movements project. (n.d.). University of Washington. https://depts.washington.edu/moves/

Milkis, S. M. (2024, April 18). *Progressivism.* Encyclopedia Britannica. https://www.britannica.com/topic/progressivism

Misinformation & fake news. (n.d.). CWU Libraries. https://libguides.lib.cwu.edu/c.php?g=625394&p=4391900

Munro, A. (2024, May 21). *Republic*. Encyclopedia Britannica. https://www.britannica.com/topic/republic-government

Pakulski, J. (n.d.). *Populism and the elite perspective*. Concilium Civitas. https://conciliumcivitas.pl/populism-and-the-elite-perspective/

Political parties, platforms, and planks. (n.d.). Teach Democracy. https://teachdemocracy.org/election-central/political-parties-platforms.html

Political Parties. (n.d.). The Library of Congress. https://www.loc.gov/classroom-materials/elections/presidential-election-process/political-parties/

Robertson, A. W. (2010). Encyclopedia of U.S. political history. Cq Press.

The effects of climate change. (n.d.). NASA. https://science.nasa.gov/climate-change/effects/

The future of democracy. (2018, October 5). International IDEA. https://www.idea.int/events/future-democracy

The purpose of political parties. (2020). Government of the Netherlands. https://www.government.nl/topics/democracy/the-purpose-of-political-parties

The United States constitution. (n.d.). National Constitution Center. https://constitutioncenter.org/the-constitution/full-text

Third parties: Role & influence. (n.d.). StudySmarter UK. https://www.studysmarter.co.uk/explanations/politics/political-participation/third-parties/

US election 2024: A really simple guide. (2024, April 19). BBC. https://www.bbc.com/news/world-us-canada-67285325

What is women's studies and why is it relevant? (2023, March 3). BestColleges. https://www.bestcolleges.com/humanities/womens-studies-programs/

What's Next Project. (2023, August 29). *What's next for American democracy?* Democracy Journal. https://democracyjournal.org/magazine/70/whats-next-for-american-democracy/

www.ingramcontent.com/pod-product-compliance
Lightning Source LLC
Chambersburg PA
CBHW070849050426
42453CB00012B/2111